Parents, Take CHARGE!

Sandy Gluckman, Ph.D.

Copyright © 2013 Sandy Gluckman

All rights reserved. No part of this book may be reproduced or transmitted in any form or by any means, electronic or mechanical, including photocopying, recording or by any information storage and retrieval system without permission from the authors, except for the inclusion of brief quotations in a review.

Design by Rock Morris
www.rockmorrisdesign.com

Illustrations: Copyright © 2013 Uros Sesum

Library of Congress Cataloging-In-Publication Data
Gluckman, Sandy
      Parents, Take Charge: Healing learning, behavior and mood challenges without medication / Sandy Gluckman
      p. cm.
Includes index.

LCCN: 2013916767
CreateSpace Independent Publishing Platform,
North Charleston, SC

BISAC: Family & Relationships / General

ISBN-10: 1491252243
ISBN-13: 978-1491252246

This book is dedicated to my husband, Merv. I could not do what I do without you. Your passion for my passion and your tireless support give me the energy to pursue my dreams.

ACKNOWLEDGEMENTS

I acknowledge and appreciate my family, Merv, Bonita, Gary, Leigh, Colin, Saul, Charlene, Avi and Janet for your love and belief in me. Thank you Bonnie and Ga for cheering me on to do this challenging work.

Grateful thanks goes also to many exceptionally talented and dedicated healthcare professionals that have inspired and taught me so much – some of whom I have worked with and others who have stretched my mind with their outstanding publications. Included are Professor Celene Bernstein, Dr. Tim Healey, Laura Kopec. Dr. Randy Naidoo, Dr. Homero Cavazos, Dr. John Demartini; Dr. Mark Hyman, Dr. Daniel Siegel, Dr. Daniel Amen, Dr. Stephen Porges, amongst many others.

Thanks to my editor, Victoria Giraud, for helping to make the book so easy to read.

Thank you dear friends, Ethel, Clea, Lane, Lauren, Shels, Celene, Nee, and Shiels for always being there for me and your enthusiastic encouragement and support.

Above all, I want to thank all the parents, teachers and children who have allowed me into their lives and in so doing, lifted my spirit, touched my heart and empowered my mind.

TABLE OF CONTENTS

Foreword ii
Introduction iv
Prologue ix

PART I
A New Look at Learning, Behavior and Mood Problems

Chapter 1   Free the Healthy Kid Inside 2
Chapter 2   Why You Should Take Charge 15
Chapter 3   From Treating Symptoms to Treating Causes 25
Chapter 4   Are Your Beliefs Keeping You Stuck? 38
Chapter 5   About the *Parents, Take Charge* Program 43

PART II
Steps 1 and 2: FIND IT and FIX IT

Chapter 6   Step 1: FIND IT 55
Chapter 7   Wired for Stress 68
Chapter 8   Who Can Help You FIND IT 77
Chapter 9   What you may FIND and how to FIX IT 88

PART III
Step 3: FIRE IT UP With NeuroParenting

Chapter 10   FIRE UP the Good. Calm the Bad 106
Chapter 11   Your NeuroParenting Toolbox – Healing Conversations 115
Chapter 12   Your NeuroParenting Toolbox – Healing Behaviors 128
Chapter 13   Mom, Dad, It Starts With You 137
Chapter 14   Parent, Heal Thyself 146
Chapter 15   Your *Parents, Take Charge* Checklist 157
Chapter 16   Are Your Values Healing or Hindering? 159
Appendix 171
About the Author 173

FOREWORD

This book will take you to a different destination, a better destination, where you can take charge. Seeing the "whole" problem - from dietary errors that negatively impact the child's individual's biochemistry, to poor capacity to rid the body of waste, to the impact of years of medication use which has buried the problem deeper - are the pieces to the puzzle that this book solves.

This book also brings to the fore a piece that is so often neglected, forgotten, or not felt to be important in the vitality and completeness of child development. The spirit of a child is the unspoken, the difficult area to discuss or put into research, or just a place where a practitioner does not want to go in the discussion of a child. Dr. Gluckman hits this area of gray matter head on in the book. Chapter 5 discusses the "life force" of a child.

The spirit is the essence of a child which begins prior to conception by the thoughts, unresolved conflict, circumstances of conception, issues during the course of the pregnancy, circumstances of the delivery, family attendance in the hospital and so much more which creates the undercurrent for that child to develop.

Foreword

I speak a lot about the "skeletons in the closet" for us as parents. I think about it from my oldest child of 9 years old to my youngest at 3 years old and how my life was so different during the conceiving of each one and where my wife and I were in our relationship and where we are now. These issues matter. This creates the undercurrent for further development of the "spirit" of a child and this will impact neurodevelopment.

As a pediatrician focused on the biomedical approach to children, it pains me when I see families who will exhaust to no end the finances and time to look at the pathology of the physical or emotional element but never for a moment, consider or give credence to the "essence or spirit" of a child. It is difficult to always put into therapeutic terms because labels that we currently have for mood disorders, adjustment disorders, anxiety, psychosis and other disorders of the mind have their root in the spirit. It's easier to give it a label, compartmentalize to an area of the brain, and then medicate or counsel that specific deficit.

In Chapter 12, Dr. Gluckman gives us a glimpse at what we do to the essence of a child when our day to day approach to life does not match up to a vital and complete spirit. None of us are perfect parents but many times the issues of our children are seen through the eyes of the "skeletons in our closet". Dr. Gluckman's short story prior to Chapter 3 is a perfect analogy to what our inadequacies are as parents and as practitioners. The team approach and continuous collaboration of us as parents with a holistic team of practitioners from the mind, the body, and the spirit will in due time take us far enough away from the tree so we can see the forest. Seeing the "whole" picture is the only way to appreciate the spirit of a child and family.

Randy Naidoo, M.D. FAAP, ABIHM

INTRODUCTION
Sandy's Story

It feels to me as though the seeds for this book were planted while I was in the womb. I was born to a wonderful mother and father. My mother had survived the holocaust but she had lost her entire family, except for one sister who she found in the United States, many years after the camps were liberated. While she was pregnant with me, my mother was struggling courageously with immense loss and grief. Knowing what I know now, I believe, that as a fetus I felt my mother's grief and pain. Feeling her pain made me enter this world with an extremely sensitive spirit that always felt stressed. Then, as an infant and young child I remember, once again, sensing my mother's hurting spirit and her pain.

Experiences of a hurting spirit – mine, and that of millions of others around me – began very early in life for me and became a theme that followed me throughout my studies and my professional career.

I was born and grew up in Johannesburg, South Africa, during the apartheid era. This was a difficult environment for a child with a sensitive spirit. Painful memories are still etched in my mind about

Introduction

the many ways in which I saw people suffer because of the shocking practices of apartheid.

My professional career began as a teacher for students in the last year of high school. In South Africa this final year of school was called Matric. I noticed how some of these eighteen year old boys and girls found the demands of their academic and social lives very stressful, while others seemed to enjoy life and cope easily. I always wondered why. Why did some students have a robust, healthy, resilient and feisty spirit and others did not? What caused this? Was it their nature? Their personality?

To find the answer to these questions I furthered my studies and obtained a Ph.D. in clinical psychology. Many years followed as I pursued a private practice as a clinical psychologist and also worked in a mental hospital. I was struck by what incredibly hurting spirits the patients all had and how their different emotional conditions were most often triggered by stress, either real or perceived.

This led me to further studies in stress, after which I facilitated stress management programs for healthcare practitioners, families and cardiac rehabilitation centers.

My interest in learning problems began with the whole brain research I completed for my doctorate. This research revealed that right brain dominant children feel great stress being educated in a left brain education system. It was difficult for them to understand and absorb and retain the information when taught in a left brain way so they were labeled as 'learning disabled.' I was incensed that these children were called 'learning disabled.' Educators, parents and psychologists did not understand that there was nothing wrong with these wonderful right brain dominant children. They simply computed the information differently. I addressed many learning conferences about the concept of 'learning disabled' being a misnomer and how this label could impact a child's spirit, self-esteem, confidence to learn and health.

Years later, further study took me into the corporate world to work with business leaders. Nelson Mandela had been released from prison and was soon to become president. Companies hired me to assist leadership to motivate and re-engage thousands of disempowered and dispirited employees. Yet again, the issue of broken spirits reared its head. It amazed me that corporate leaders could expect employees with such hurting spirits to be committed, loyal, and productive as well as generate exceptional results!

My experiences as a teacher, psychologist and leadership coach taught me one powerful lesson: A healthy, happy spirit is the key to physical, mental, emotional and social well-being. A strong, healthy spirit promotes a healthy body and brain. A hurting spirit affects every aspect of our being. I saw this recurring theme in all the students, patients, business leaders and employees that I worked with.

Now I see the same recurring theme in millions of children that have learning, behavior and mood challenges. These children have a hurting spirit that is affecting their body and brain. Treating these academic, behavior and emotional symptoms with medication is not the answer. In *Parents, Take Charge*, I suggest that the answer is to begin the treatment at the point where these problems all begin – with the hurting spirit. (As you read further you will note that in this book spirit refers to the *core of our being* and is not a religious concept).

In 1998 my husband and I immigrated to the United States. Some years after my arrival in the USA, I attended a healthcare conference and heard a remarkable man, Dr. Tim Healey, give a remarkable talk about

Introduction

the effect of stress on the spirit and physiology of children and how this can trigger learning, behavior and mood problems. I remember feeling my heart pounding, and I knew that for the next chapter of my career I wanted to work with these children and their parents and teachers. Thus the *Parents, Take Charge* and *Teachers, Take Charge* programs were born.

Thank you for joining me on this quest to help children be everything they are capable of being. I would love to hear from you. Please visit me at my website and tell me and other parents about your *Parents, Take Charge* journey.

What You Will Read in This Book

Please Note: I use the "he" and "she" pronouns interchangeably. In some places I use "he" and in other place "she." There is no specific reason for this other than an attempt to be politically correct.

This book provides information as well as tools for healing your children. It can be used as a handbook and guide on a daily basis. In Part I, I explain why I call the program *Parents, Take Charge* and why it is so important for parents, today, to *Take Charge* of healing their kids. We explore the question that is on the lips of so many parents today – *should I medicate or not medicate my child?* You will learn about functional medicine and how this is revolutionizing the treatment of children with learning, behavior and mood problems. Chapter 5 introduces you to how the drug-free *Parents, Take Charge* Program works and why it is getting such excellent results.

Part II highlights why the child's spirit-body-brain must be treated as ONE system and shows you how to do this using the 3-Step *Parents, Take Charge* Program. You will read about your role in the healing process. A detailed case study demonstrates exactly how the program works. I explain the role of stress in the development of your child's learning, behavior and mood problems and why your child may be more vulnerable to stress than others.

Part III is the parenting skills and tools section of the book. This is your toolbox. I offer eight healing parenting tools that I call NeuroParenting. These tools stimulate your child's healthy spirit-body-brain chemistry. NeuroParenting tools are fun to use and can be easily applied to your interactions with your kids on a daily basis. Finally in Part III, you read about how to ensure your own spirit-body-brain health.

The 3-step *Parents, Take Charge* program, when intentionally applied, will build a foundation for a lifetime of health and well-being for your children and for your family.

PROLOGUE

Let me tell you about David…

David is a sweet, funny, friendly eleven-year-old who has been through a very tough time since he was six years old. He has been described as unmotivated, an underachiever, lazy, defiant, a perfectionist, hyperactive and disruptive by his teachers and parents. Over the past several years, he has been diagnosed by different healthcare specialists as having ADHD, OCD, ODD, and depression. With each new diagnosis came a new medication.

Each time I looked into David's big brown eyes, I could see his spirit was hurting, and that he was confused and sad because all he wanted was to be able to learn easily, have fun with other kids, enjoy life and feel good about himself. He just wanted to be a carefree six-year-old as all six-year-olds should be.

David's mother was convinced the doctors were missing something. She intuitively knew that underneath the layers of problems David was grappling with, there existed a healthy, normal, talented, highly intelligent and creative boy. Finally, after six years of a heartbreaking search bolstered by her own courage and determination, Mom found a healthcare practitioner who confirmed her intuitive sense that the other doctors had indeed missed something.

This practitioner found that David was an anxious, sensitive child with low self-confidence and self-belief. He also discovered that David had high levels of fungus in his intestines, low levels of vitamins A, E, C and CoQ10; low magnesium, deficiency in B vitamins, high stress markers and a gluten intolerance. These irregularities were responsible for David's troubling symptoms. The learning, behavior and mood problems he grappled with were not ADHD, OCD, ADD or depression, but were symptoms of what was happening in David's digestive system and other parts of his body. The high stress indicators, vitamin deficiencies and intolerance to gluten would explain his irritability, emotional meltdowns, low energy levels, poor motivation and difficulty with focus and attention.

David's new doctor explained to his mom that his symptoms were all easily treatable. Each of the identified biological causes was treated. David was given an anti-fungal; he was given the supplements his body was missing and gluten was eliminated from his diet. Counseling was a very important aspect of the treatment plan to heal David's hurting spirit and improve his belief in himself. He had taken a severe emotional battering from all the negative feedback he had been getting from his parents, teachers and even peers. The ultimate goal of David's treatment plan was to restore the natural ability of his *spirit, body and brain to function effectively together – without prescription drugs.*

Nine months later, David's symptoms were almost gone. His grades improved dramatically, and his natural leadership abilities emerged. He understood and practiced healthy nutrition and he had vastly improved levels of energy. He interacted well with his peers and made some special friends. He even learned how to play a mean piano.

What about the diagnoses of all those doctors? How could they all be so wrong? What did this healthcare practitioner do differently to restore David to balanced health and wellness? How was he able to do what others failed to do? Why did David have to endure many years of unsuccessful treatments, which gave him little or no relief and sent him on a terrible emotional rollercoaster ride?

David's story is the story of literally millions of children, except for one fact - *in too many cases these children continue to struggle because healthcare professionals treating them are masking the outward symptoms with medication instead of looking for the actual source of the problems.* Sadly, the traditional approach of treating the symptoms with medication leaves the true underlying causes of the problem undetected and untreated, which means these children will never be healed. They will always need medication to help them manage their symptoms. Eventually, they will become adults on medication because traditional medicine has not helped them identify and remove the real reasons for their problems.

Does David's story describe the story of your child?

- Is your child another David?
- Do you know a child like David?
- Have you been going from one healthcare practitioner to another looking for answers?
- Are you dissatisfied with the results of the treatment your child is getting?

- Do you believe that the practitioners you have seen for your child are missing something?
- Are you resisting the idea of medication but don't know what else to do?
- Are you giving your child medication each day with a heavy heart?
- Is your child on medication? Would you like to find a way of weaning him or her off medication to avoid long-term dependency?

The goal of *Parents, Take Charge* is to introduce you to a new way of *healing* children's learning, behavior or mood problems, safely and effectively. You will learn about the latest research, and read case studies and stories that show the powerful benefits of this drug-free *Parents, Take Charge* Program.

This book is for all parents who yearn for their children to feel good about themselves, to be healthy, have confidence, act with courage and relate well to others. It is for all parents who are looking for a way to help their children learn easily, use their talents and love life! *Just like David!*

In this book you will learn how to make this happen.

PART I

CHAPTER 1
Free the Healthy Kid Inside

The Creator gathered all of Creation and said, "I want to hide something from the humans until they are ready for it. It is the realization that they create their own reality."

The eagle said, "Give it to me, I will take it to the moon."

The Creator said, "No. One day they will go there and find it."

The salmon said, "I will bury it on the bottom of the ocean."

"No. They will go there too."

The buffalo said, "I will bury it on the Great Plains."

The Creator said, "They will cut into the skin of the Earth and find it even there."

Grandmother Mole, who lives in the breast of Mother Earth, and who has no physical eyes but sees with spiritual eyes, said, "Put it inside of them."

And the Creator said, "It is done."

Are you looking "inside" to find the real cause of your child's symptoms?

Let's Free the Healthy Kid Inside!

David's story is the perfect example of what I witness over and over again – that behind the layers of learning, behavior and mood issues that so many children grapple with, there is a problem-free child with a healthy spirit, body and brain. Martha Herbert states this thought beautifully in her book, The Autism Revolution, where she writes, "Your child is in there."

If you are a mom or dad, it is vitally important that you know this truth, and you believe it, with every fiber of your being!

Your healthy, happy, talented child is "in there."

Start with a Vision

If you want to liberate the healthy child within, who is currently locked in by all kinds of difficult symptoms, then you *MUST* change the way you see your child. Instead of seeing problems, see potential. Instead of seeing crises, see learning moments. Instead of seeing dysfunction, see creativity. Instead of seeing disease, see health. Instead of seeing so much that is wrong, see so much that is right. Instead of seeing *can't*, see *can*. If you do not have this mental picture in your mind of your healthy, happy, talented child in *there*, then all you will focus on are the problems *out here*. All you will see, day after day is a child who is struggling to be okay because you believe, "There is something wrong" with him or her.

The problem is that most mainstream healthcare practitioners do not see the healthy child within. Your doctors don't tell you that your child with great potential is *in there* – because this observation goes against their training. Traditional doctors are trained to be disease-focused, so they will look at the symptoms, diagnose the so-called disease or disorder, then pull out their prescription pad and use prescribed medication as the preferred form of treatment. Their goal is to contain the symptoms. All children presenting with the same symptoms will get the same diagnosis and the same medication. These healthcare practitioners don't see the child with the enormous potential; they only see what they consider to be an unhealthy child who has walked into their consulting room. Unfortunately, their disease-focused attitude influences parents and educators to approach the child's challenges in the same limited way.

Sadly, while we continue to unsuccessfully do what we've always done, millions of wonderful children are waiting for us to do something different that will finally free them to be all they were born to be.

Moms and Dads, it is time for you to rise up and

Take Charge!

YOU can free your Children!

A Walk in the Moccasins of Parents

A huge amount of time, money, energy and emotion is spent by parents wanting to help children overcome their learning, behavior or mood problems. Yet, far too often, the problems persist, sometimes to a lesser degree, but most often they do not go away.

With the very best intentions, parents will take their children from doctor to psychologist, from psychologist to psychiatrist, to yet another medical specialist. They will try occupational and physical therapy, perhaps biofeedback, sensory integration, behavior modification, or equine therapy, among many therapies, hoping that one of these will be the magic bullet. Certainly these therapies can be extremely beneficial, provided that the right therapy is introduced into the child's treatment plan at the right time, for the right reason. (More about this in chapter 8).

Children with these problems notice Mom and Dad's stressed, worried and anxious faces. What else are they to believe other than they are the cause; they are a disappointment; there is something wrong with them; they cannot learn or behave like their peers.

A Modern-day Epidemic of Learning, Behavior and Mood Problems in Children

The numbers of children with diagnoses like ADD, ADHD, OCD, ODD, Depression, Asperger's, Tourette's and Autism, for example, is truly staggering. Statistics from professional journals, research institutes and the Centers for Disease Control (CDC) show that sixteen million children have been diagnosed with a learning problem. One in every five school-age children is diagnosed with a social, emotional or learning problem. It is predicted that these numbers will continue to increase. The statistics show there is a correlation between learning disabilities and depression, anxiety, substance abuse and suicide.

Psychotropic and stimulant drugs have been the treatment of choice. Millions of children with learning, behavior and mood challenges have been medicated over the last two decades and the number of prescriptions being written continues to escalate at an alarming pace. The 2013 CDC data (Center for Disease Control in the USA) show, for example, that an estimated 6.4 million children, ages four through seventeen, have received an ADHD diagnosis at some point in their lives – a 53% rise in the past decade. About two-thirds of those with a current diagnosis receive prescriptions for stimulants such as Ritalin and Adderall. In 30 years there has been a twenty-fold increase in the consumption of drugs for attention-deficit disorder.

And yet children are not being healed.

The traditional medical approach is clearly unable to heal and free the children or stop this epidemic. It seems to me that the existing medication-driven, disease-focused, one-size-fits-all treatment approach, practiced by many traditional healthcare practitioners, is one of the factors that contribute to these staggering numbers of learning, behavior and mood problems in kids of all ages. As a result, children are carrying these problems into their teens and adulthood. About 60% of children with ADHD become adults with ADHD, which translates into 4% of the US adult population, or 8 million adults. These unresolved problems have a profoundly negative effect on their lives, on our society and on the economy.

To Medicate? Or Not to Medicate?

Clearly, using medication is a highly contentious issue and one that causes parents, healthcare practitioners and educators to have heated disagreements. I am opposed to medication as the first line of treatment. I strongly advocate using medication as a *last resort* and not the automatic and immediate knee-jerk response for a child who has cognitive, behavior or mood symptoms.

In fact, I am *not totally opposed* to medication. Traditional medicine certainly has a role to play, particularly in treating acute medical conditions. For children who display cognitive, behavior and mood symptoms on the severe end of the continuum, a combination of the drug and drug-free approaches may be necessary. In his book, *The UltraMind Solution*, Dr. Mark Hyman writes, *Our goal in medicine should be to find the right 'medicine' for each person, without prejudice, whether it is a drug, a nutrient, diet change, detoxification, a hormone, exercise, or exorcism!* While there may be times when medication can be useful for treating certain learning, behavior and mood symptoms, I see medication as being the exception rather than the rule.

For parents, it comes down to being able to answer these questions:

1. Do I want to get to the bottom of, and put an end to, my child's problems? Am I willing to do whatever it takes to remove the problems he or she struggles with, even if the solution is unlikely to include prescribed medication?

OR

2. Do I want to use medication that will suppress these problems? Will I agree with a solution that will hide, but not heal, the

problem? Am I okay knowing this solution is, most likely, a short-term answer rather than a long-term solution?

A Special Note for Parents Who Have Chosen to Medicate

If you are a parent giving your child medication and happy with the positive changes in your child's life, don't feel offended by my point of view. I do not judge your decision as being bad or wrong. My philosophy is that medication should be a last resort, but whatever your reasons may be for choosing to medicate, I respect and honor that your decision feels right for you in your circumstances. I do believe that you and your child can still benefit greatly from the information I am sharing with you in this book. Read further and use those parts of the book that, together with the medication, can enhance your life and your child's health and healing.

Parents who use the *Parents, Take Charge* Program do so because:

1. They have made the decision to heal their child by going drug-free.
2. They have tried medication, but had a negative reaction.
3. Their child's personality changes with medication.
4. Their child is already on medication and they want to prepare for a time when they can wean him or her off a long-term dependency.
5. Their children have no problems. These parents are using the program preventatively to maintain the health and well-being of the family.

Consider These Facts about Medication

For some children, the short-term impact of medication seems so positive that parents tend to block out any thoughts about long-term implications. They just want the symptoms to go away so that their child can be happy, which is completely understandable. Medicating children can be a huge relief for parents, particularly if you believe, as I do, that a parent is only as happy as their unhappiest child. Oh, the joy of hearing that your child is doing well at school, of watching them make friends, having less upheavals at home and having to deal with fewer meltdowns. *So, why wouldn't parents choose to medicate? Why would a parent even consider the drug-free option?*

Here are some of these reasons:

1. There is something happening somewhere in the child's body that is the actual root cause for their learning, behavior and mood problems, but nobody is looking for the true cause. When you medicate the externally evident symptoms, the real underlying root cause of the problems remains untreated. Drugs, therefore, are often a band-aid, a short-term solution to mask the symptoms. The unidentified underlying causes can continue to aggravate existing symptoms, cause new symptoms to develop and eventually can reduce the effectiveness of the drugs.

2. We do not yet know the long-term biomedical and neurochemical effects of many of the drugs children take for learning, behavior and mood problems. The preliminary results of a research study were reported at the 2012 Pediatric Academic Societies meeting in Boston. These results show that for the ten top pediatric conditions, children accounted for 60% of patients but only 12% of the clinical drug trials. These facts are pretty scary when you consider that decisions about drug

treatment for children should be based on clear evidence of the safety and effectiveness of these drugs for kids. Understandably though, parents do not want to submit their children to drug tests.

3. Not only are children stigmatized by diagnostic labels, which suggest there is something "wrong with them," but they also learn that if you have a problem, you take a tablet to fix it. This kind of "training" and belief system will, most likely, follow them into adulthood. They will then teach their children the same message, which is good news for doctors and pharmaceutical companies but very bad news for millions of children and adults. When the treatment of choice is medication, children are unlikely to learn the truth that there is nothing "wrong" with them and that their symptoms can be fixed in healthy ways.

4. The effects of stimulants on children with attention problems have been shown to fade over time. Research indicates that attention-deficit drugs increase concentration in the short term, but when given to children over long periods of time, they do not improve school achievement, academic performance, peer relationships or behavior problems. A report on a comprehensive follow-up study at Montreal Children's Hospital discovered that... *At the end of five years, hyperkinetic children who received drugs (either Ritalin or Chloropromazine) did not differ significantly from children who had not received the drugs. Although it appeared that hyperactive children treated with Ritalin were initially more manageable, the degree of improvement and emotional adjustment were essentially identical at the end of*

five years to that seen in a group of children who had received no medication at all.

5. Many children suffer physical and emotional side effects that make life even harder for them. Some of the known side effects for stimulants include loss of appetite, weight loss, insomnia, reduced stature, tics, "zombie" demeanor, stomach aches, serious vision problems, mood or behavior changes, seizures, confusion, respiratory and cardiac effects.

6. The drugs prescribed for ADHD/ADD are closely related to some illegal street drugs. These include dextroamphetamine (street name, "dexies"), methamphetamine (street name, crystal meth) and cocaine. In his book, *ADHD: Drug-free and Doin' Fine*, Dr. Lawrence Weathers writes: *It is indeed an irony that we imprison people for making or selling drugs that are very similar to the drugs we prescribe for ADHD children.*

    A research report in the "Archives of General Psychiatry" states, *Cocaine, which is one of the most reinforcing and addicting of the abused drugs, has pharmacological actions that are very similar to those of methylphenidate (Ritalin, Concerta), which is now the most commonly prescribed psychotropic medicine for children in the U.S.*

7. The medications work as long as you continue to give them to the child. The drug may help kids, *while they are taking it*, by reducing inattention, impulsivity and hyperactivity so they are able to function better, but the drugs do not *heal or cure the problem.*

8. Stimulant drugs enhance the child's ability to concentrate (especially on tasks that the child finds uninteresting or boring or when they are anxious and frustrated) but they don't improve broader learning abilities.

9. A high percentage of those who are being medicated develop long-term dependency on these drugs and many may gravitate to non-prescription harder drugs.

Medication Can Drug the Spirit of the Child you are Trying to Free!

If there were only one reason to use medication as a last resort, for me, it would be this reason: *The drugs prescribed for learning, behavior and mood challenges can chemically blunt the child's spirit.** Some children become quiet and subdued. Parents often use the words "robot-like" or "zombie" to describe how their child appears on medication. Others say they see a personality change in the child.

For kids to be resilient, courageous and determined, they will need a healthy, strong and vibrant spirit. They need a strong spirit to help them build positive self-belief and a clear sense of their unique identity. They need a robust spirit to help them feel good about themselves, be proud of whom they are and to recognize and use their unique talents. Children with dulled medicated spirits will find it difficult to become self-confident, bold, independent thinkers who are successful in life.

Many children are aware of feeling dulled. They complain that they don't like the way the medication makes them feel. Some courageous and determined children even refuse to continue to take their meds, or even resort to pretending to take it. With the best of intentions, some parents and teachers are so focused on wanting the child to achieve good grades and behave like all the other "normal" children that they insist the child take medication. Yes, many kids on medication can indeed focus and pay attention and their grades do improve. But the price they may pay for this medication is a spirit that is dulled. They feel disconnected from the power of their true spirit.

* In this book "spirit" is defined as the essence of who we are at the core of our being.

Labels are Destructive

The diagnoses that accompany medication also present a problem. How can we expect young children or teenagers to feel special, find true self-confidence and inner strength when they have been stigmatized by labels such as ADD, OCD, ADHD, ODD and told they have a disorder? The label, unfortunately, makes the child special but in a negative way. It identifies them as "having problems," which is not the kind of specialness and identity children need.

Feeling special should be a feeling that comes from the child's inner spirit. The problem is that medication blunts the child's ability to connect with the magical, powerful, spirited person that he or she really is.

You Have a Choice

In this book I will introduce you to a new and successful way of treating learning, behavior and mood challenges, that is label-free and medication-free. Traditional healthcare does not offer this option, nor will most practitioners tell you about such an option, usually because they are uninformed and do not know enough about it. This book will empower you with everything you need to know about this healthy new way of treating the problems your child is grappling with. With this knowledge, you will be in a strong position to make the decision about your child's treatment that feels right for you.

In the chapters that follow, I will show you how the *Parents, Take Charge* Program has the potential to *eradicate your* child's symptoms. I offer you information, the step-by-step roadmap and the tools to enable you to *Take Charge* of healing your child.

CHAPTER 2
Why You Should *Take Charge*

That's the Way We Do Things Around Here.

An interesting and enlightening experiment using monkeys was performed in 1967. Five monkeys were locked in a cage, a banana was hung from the top of the cage, and a ladder was placed right underneath it. As predicted, one of the monkeys immediately raced toward the ladder to grab the banana. As soon as he started to climb, the researcher sprayed the monkey with ice-cold water and also sprayed the other four monkeys.

When a second monkey tried to climb the ladder, the researcher sprayed that monkey with ice-cold water, as well as the other four monkeys that were watching. This pattern was repeated again and again until the monkeys learned their lesson – climbing equals scary cold water for everyone, so no one climbs the ladder.

Once the five monkeys knew the drill, the researcher replaced one of the monkeys with a new inexperienced one. As predicted, the new monkey spotted the banana, and headed for the ladder. The other four monkeys, knowing the drill, jumped on the new monkey and beat him up. The injured novice soon learned – No climbing the ladder and No Banana. Period – without ever being sprayed with water!

When the scientist replaced a second monkey with a new one, the events repeated themselves – monkey runs toward the ladder; other monkeys beat him up; new monkey does not attempt to climb again – with one notable detail: the first new monkey, who had never received the cold-water treatment himself, would, with equal vigor and enthusiasm, join in beating the new guy on the block.

When the researcher replaced a third monkey, the same thing happened; likewise for the fourth and fifth, until, eventually, all the monkeys had been replaced and none of the ones in the cage had any experience or knowledge of the cold-water treatment. None of them knew why they could not get the banana. All they knew was… *that's the way we do things around here.*

Is your child's healthcare practitioner clinging to the past – saying that's the way we do things around here?

It Has to Do With Change

Did you ever have one of those tube-shaped toys called a kaleidoscope? You looked through the opening at the top and saw a beautiful display of colors, patterns and designs. Then, as you twisted the bottom of the tube, you watched as the colors and patterns transformed and changed into different colors and different patterns. Because we are living in a time of immense change accompanied by mind-boggling scientific, medical and technological advances, today's world seems like one of those kaleidoscopes. Yet with all this progress, something strange is happening. In spite of the incredible medical progress and advancement, millions of children continue to suffer with learning, behavior and mood symptoms that hold them back from being the best they can be academically, emotionally and socially. And the numbers are growing each day. Why?

I believe these problems are reaching epidemic proportions because of how change happens. Have you noticed that whenever there is change of any kind, there are two different types of responses? Some people love it; they are inspired by the new ways and become early adopters. Others hold on tightly to the way it has always been, resisting the change with all their might, offering every possible argument why the proposed change is not a good thing. Until the new way eventually becomes the accepted way, there is a struggle between those who say, "That's the way we've always done it," and those who say, "That doesn't work anymore."

This struggle between old and new is happening today in healthcare.

A New Era of Medicine

Healthcare is in the process of being reinvented. An exciting new era of medicine is emerging. There is *a new generation of healthcare practitioners* who recognize the limitations of conventional medicine. These modern practitioners are revolutionizing the treatment of children with learning, behavior and mood challenges with a groundbreaking treatment approach referred to as *functional medicine*, which is the fastest growing field in medicine today. Functional medicine is transforming the lives of children and their families by creating health and healing. Although these functional practitioners may come from different fields of healthcare (pediatricians, psychologists, chiropractors, psychiatrists, nutritionists, neurologists, gastroenterologists and endocrinologists), they all have one thing in common – they all practice the basic scientific principle of functional medicine:

Find and fix the root cause of the problem – don't medicate the symptoms.

Functional medicine heals children by finding and treating the underlying causes of the learning, behavior and mood problems. This practice is vastly different from managing and masking the problems with medication, but not knowing *why* the child has the problem in the first place. There can be no true healing when you do not treat the actual cause.

Although now proven to be highly effective, but because functional medicine is still relatively new, some mainstream healthcare practitioners still cling tightly to the traditional, conventional way of doing things. Or perhaps it is simply that they do not like change or that they are not open-minded enough to learn about the new approach. Whatever the reason, some defensive traditional healthcare practitioners regard the latest research with suspicion and refuse to see that too often the conventional approach is no longer working for the patient. They cannot see that in the case of learning, behavior and mood symptoms, the conventional approach can often cause more problems than it solves.

This is the struggle between the old and the new and parents can get caught in the crossfire.

Asking *Why?* Versus Asking *What?*

The staggering numbers of children struggling with academic, emotional and social problems is the result of parents and practitioners asking the wrong question. They are asking, *"WHAT condition does this child have?"* instead of, *"WHY is this happening to this particular child, in this particular way, at this particular time in his or her life?"*

When We Ask the What Question

When a parent or healthcare practitioner asks, *"WHAT condition does this child have?"* their focus is on the particular cluster of external symptoms they are seeing. These symptoms are given a diagnostic label which is, most often, followed by a prescription. Millions of children

presenting with similar symptoms will get the same diagnosis and the same prescription. This practice keeps doctors very busy and the pharmaceutical companies very profitable but it is a form of medicine proving to be remarkably limited and unhelpful for kids with learning, behavior and mood issues because they do not find and fix the cause. In addition, the diagnosis becomes a label that hangs around the child's neck forever. Millions of children today have a learning, behavior or mood label that stigmatizes them and eventually becomes an unfortunate part of their identity that follows them into adulthood.

When We Ask the Why Question

When a healthcare practitioner or parent asks, *"Why is this happening in this child?"* the focus will be on finding and treating *the underlying root cause* of the externally visible symptoms. The functional approach to the treatment of cognitive and behavioral problems in children is truly life-changing. Healing symptoms by finding and removing the underlying cause can make the difference between children enjoying life or struggling with life. It can make the difference between children carrying a heavy emotional burden or being young and carefree. It can make the difference between having a long-term dependency on medication versus having their problems eradicated and being able to

tap into their true potential. Using functional medicine to eliminate the symptoms can make an immense difference for those children who struggle with these problems day after day, year after year, believing that they cannot be helped. The idea of treating the root cause instead of medicating the symptoms came from forward-thinking practitioners who dared to ask the *Why?* Question: *Why is this happening to this particular child, in this particular way, at this particular time in the child's life?*

> *This kind of healthcare practitioner healed David, whom you met in the Prologue of this book. This kind of healthcare practitioner is one you want for your child!*

Dr. Mark Hyman, a practicing MD and author of, *The Ultramind Solution*, is one of the world's leaders in the field of functional medicine. He writes, "In the future every doctor will be a functional medicine doctor. It will be the only way that healthcare will be practiced." I agree. It will, however, take many years before this change from the old to the new becomes standard practice. In the meantime, parents will need to *Take Charge!* and become informed about this new treatment option.

I am not suggesting that practitioners are deliberately misleading parents or being unethical in their approach. I am concerned that some traditional practitioners have not kept up-to-date with the dramatic discoveries during the last fifteen years in the field of learning, behavior and mood challenges in children. They are unaware of, or disinterested in the fact that new information has shattered many of our traditional beliefs about diagnosing and treating such problems. Many parents tell me that their mainstream doctors are cynical naysayers when they present them with this new information and research. That is why *YOU* need to *Take Charge*. It is also why I feel driven to empower you with an understanding of the possible real reasons behind your children's problems and enable you to seek options that can offer true healing.

What Does This New Era of Medicine Mean for Parents?

Just this ...

You are faced with a vitally important decision. *Do you use the traditional treatment approach, the new functional medicine approach or a combination of both to help your children overcome their learning, behavior or mood challenges?* You want the very best treatment solution for your child. In order to help your child the safest and most effective way possible, You will need to know how to choose the right practitioner for your child, know what to ask for and what to expect. Doctors of all disciplines, just like every other profession, can be great, good or bad. Remember, they work for you! But you must know what kind of doctor you are looking for and why.

My goal with this book is to inform you about this new way of identifying and treating the learning, behavior and mood problems your children grapple with. With a comprehensive understanding of what this new option offers, you can then make an informed decision. The chapters in Part I show you how the functional treatment approach differs from the treatment approach practiced by traditional healthcare practitioners. You will also learn about the *Parents, Take Charge* Program. After reading Part I, if you do decide to follow the functional approach to treat your child, Parts II and III of the book will guide you in the step-by-step process to successfully put this into practice and begin *healing your child's symptoms*.

Let's be Open-Minded

Albert Einstein was not only a man of great accomplishments but also a man of wise words. These quotes from his writings give us a message that we all need to hear in these times of great change:

> "The only thing that interferes with my learning is my education."
>
> "I am neither especially clever nor especially gifted. I am only very, very curious."
>
> "I believe in standardizing automobiles, not human beings."
>
> "Insanity is doing the same thing over and over again and expecting different results."
>
> "Great spirits have always found violent opposition from mediocre minds."

I am not sure whether this is what Einstein intended, but I think there is an unspoken message in these words of wisdom. Could it be something like... *let's be open-minded?*

Learning, behavior and mood problems in children and adults have skyrocketed. There is too much ego and politics interfering with doing what is right for our children. We see this in the dismissive attitude of some traditional practitioners who prefer to continue to do what they have always done when treating children with these challenges, although the results are dismal. We see ego and politics at play in the billions of dollars pharmaceutical companies make from selling medications for kids; we even see ego and politics in education where some schools and teachers encourage parents to medicate their children so that it is easier to teach them.

And I want to shout out... *Hey! This is not about you! It's about our children. It's about giving the next generation and the generations that follow, everything they need to flourish in the challenging 21st century. So let's get together with open minds and explore how we can actually* **heal** *these children!*

Like Einstein, the modern practitioners of functional medicine are saying:

- Let's not keep doing what's not working.
- Let's not be hostage to what we learnt in our education.
- Let's look at this problem differently.
- Let's not allow ego-driven, defensive nay-sayers to hold us back or minimize the amazing worth of what we offer.
- Let's free the wonderful children of their symptoms.

PARENTS, TAKE CHARGE!

There is a *Take Charge* Movement Happening

Parents everywhere are beginning to rise up and *Take Charge!* They are saying, "Enough! We want to know why our beloved children are hurting this way. We want to know what is causing our children to feel this way and behave this way. We do not want just a quick-fix or a band-aid solution. We want to find a way to *permanently remove* these symptoms."

> Do you feel the same way?
>
> Have you tried many different treatment solutions with only marginal success?
>
> Has there been no significant improvement in, or eradication of, the child's symptoms?

Then it sounds like you are ready to know more about how to permanently remove your child's current symptoms. In the remaining chapters of Part I, you will learn:

- How functional medicine heals.
- What we mean by a root cause.
- Why the *Parents, Take Charge* Program is so effective.
- The benefits of this new approach for your child.
- Possible root causes your child may have.
- Who can help you identify your child's root causes.
- How to identify the right healthcare practitioner/s.
- What your new role is in healing your child.
- What you will need to do differently as the parent.

CHAPTER 3
From Treating Symptoms to Treating Causes

Have You Heard this Enlightening Elephant Story?

One day five blind men, who knew nothing of elephants, examined one to learn what it was. Each was told to touch it in a different spot. One man touched the side, one an ear, one a leg, one a tusk and one the trunk. After a while, when each was satisfied that he now knew the true nature of the animal, they all sat down for a discussion.

"We now know that the elephant is like a wall," said the one who touched the side. "The evidence is conclusive."

"I believe you are mistaken, sir," said the one who touched an ear. "The elephant is more like a large fan."

"You are both wrong!" said the leg man. "The creature is obviously much like a tree."

"A tree?" questioned the tusk-toucher. "How can you mistake a spear for a tree?"

"What!" said the trunk-feeler. "A spear is long and round, but anyone knows it doesn't move."

"Couldn't you feel the muscles? It's definitely a type of snake! Even a blind man could see that!" declared the fifth blind man.

The argument grew more heated, and finally escalated into a battle, for each of the five believed he had the only answer, because none of them could see the whole elephant.

Does your child's doctor see the whole child? Or does he just see just the parts he wants to see?

How Functional Medicine Differs from Mainstream Medicine

Traditional Medicine
1. Treats all parts of the body as separate
2. Treats symptoms
3. Disease-centered
- One-size-fits-all treatment
4. Relies on a diagnosis/label
- Treats the label

Functional Medicine
1. Treats body and brain as ONE integrated system
2. Treats underlying root causes
3. Patient-centered
- Personalized treatment
4. No labels
- Treats what's not working

Let's explore these differences.

1. Treats Body and Brain as ONE System

The functional practitioner treats the body and brain as one *integrated system* that functions through complex web-like interactions of many systems. A breakdown in any one organ or biological system will trigger a series of breakdowns in other related organs and systems - like a house of cards. Dramatic scientific discoveries during the last ten to twenty years have shown, for example, that immune system dysfunction, chronic infection, gastrointestinal issues and detoxification problems play a central role in causing the learning, behavioral and mood symptoms so many children struggle with. These discoveries challenge the conventional belief that the body is made up of independent, separately functioning parts.

Heavy metal toxicity, often found in children's bodies, is just one example of how the body and brain are one system. Each toxic molecule creates a cascade of reactions, like ripples in a pond, interfering with normal physiology and disrupting many brain functions. Some of the symptoms caused by toxicity are skin or sinus problems, fatigue and bloating, constipation, headaches, muscle or joint pain and feeling down. Each child's symptoms will be dependent on that child's genetic, constitutional and emotional vulnerabilities. Heavy metal toxicity can also be related to symptoms of learning, behavior and mood problems. Research shows that children with even mildly elevated lead levels can suffer from a reduced IQ, attention deficit and poor school performance. Lead is considered to be the leading culprit in toxin-caused hyperactivity. It is not uncommon to find mercury toxicity in children with learning, behavior and mood challenges. Toxic levels of mercury can cause malabsorption of vitamins and minerals. It can affect concentration, memory and language abilities, as well as fine motor and visual spatial skills. In his book, *Clean*, Dr. Alexandro Junger writes, "Mercury ... is known as the great mimicker." Mercury toxicity can present as almost any other disease.

Diagnosing the body and brain as one system will provide the answer to the question, "Why does my child have these symptoms?" Remember David from the Prologue? A combination of malfunctions – intestinal fungus, vitamin deficiencies, high stress levels, gluten intolerance and low self-esteem – contributed to David's neurotransmitters being off balance. This contributed to his irritability, emotional meltdowns, low energy levels, poor motivation and difficulty with focus and attention. The neurologist, psychologist and psychiatrist David visited, each looked at him through the lens of their particular area of specialization. None of them treated David's body and brain as one system. As a result, they did not discover the real source of David's problems and could not eliminate his symptoms.

2. Treats Underlying Root Causes

Fix the real problem and the symptoms go away.

The goal of functional medicine is to identify and address the root causes of the child's problems. Functional practitioners do not believe that the learning, behavior or mood problems are the real problem. They see these as being symptoms of an unidentified root cause. These problems are really just messengers telling us there is an underlying root cause waiting to be identified and treated. When the child has a health, learning, mood or behavior problem, think of it as the child's way of telling you, "Mom, Dad, teacher, something is not working; something needs fixing. I need you to find out what is causing me to feel and behave in this way. I do not need you to drug me. I need you to 'listen' to what my problems are really trying to tell you."

What Exactly is a Root Cause?

In the context of this book, a root cause is a malfunction *anywhere* in the human system that sets up a chain of other malfunctions that eventually trigger symptoms that look like learning, behavior or mood disorders. Mainstream medicine believes a specific symptom indicates a specific problem in a specific part of the body or brain. Functional practitioners will investigate the health of *all* major systems and organs in the body, looking for the root of the child's learning, behavior and mood challenges. Most conventional doctors would not do this search because it goes against their belief that the body is made up of separately functioning parts.

The challenge for functional practitioners is that, although the observable symptoms may look the same from one child to the next, the underlying root cause can be different. For example, in one child the attention and concentration problems could be related to problems in the digestive system. In another child, the same attention and concentration problems could be a result of vitamin and mineral deficiencies. In yet another child, the cause could be heavy metal toxicity – or a combination of some of the above. Compared to many traditional practitioners, functional practitioners take a far more comprehensive history-taking, which provides the clues they are looking for regarding the possible origins of the problems.

Finding and fixing the root causes for each child results in true healing. To be able to discover and follow the trail of breakdowns in the child's body and brain, the healthcare practitioner would need to know how the entire human system works. They would need to have whole body diagnostic and testing skills. Most traditional practitioners often have diagnostic and testing skills only in a specific area of specialization.

3. Patient-Centered Care

Your Child is One of a Kind. I want to get to know everything about him.

To discover and treat the particular root cause in each child, the practitioner will treat every child as a one-of-a-kind case. (Although I am writing about functional medicine as it applies to children, exactly the same approach applies to any person, young or old.) This kind of care is truly personalized medicine, and it is what makes functional medicine so remarkable. Each child is regarded as being totally unique – with unique symptoms, unique needs, a unique story and requiring a unique treatment plan. Functional practitioners look at the possible personal contributing factors and background of each child – genetic makeup, signs of poor diet, lack of essential nutrients, emotional stress, environmental toxins, lack of exercise and other personal lifestyle issues… The story this information tells will answer the "why" question. An individualized treatment plan is then devised to treat that child.

To offer such personalized treatment, these practitioners spend a great deal more time with their patients than the average mainstream doctor does. The practice of this kind of personalized medicine is vastly different from disease-centered medicine, with less time given to each individual patient. Studies show visits with mainstream doctors can average about twenty minutes; doctors tend to change the subject back to technical talk when patients mention their emotions; they interrupt patients' initial statements after twenty-three seconds on average and they spend one minute providing information. Most functional practitioners have a patient-centered outlook; they involve the child and the parents in the healing process and display lots of care and attention. They respond quickly to phone calls and offer lots of advice and a compassionate ear. Also, by listening to the patient and learning his or her story, the practitioner brings the child and the parents into the discovery and treatment process, empowering them to be partners in healing the child. This *individualized patient* care makes patients feel important and understood compared to the impersonal one-size-fits-all mainstream approach. This kind of doctor-patient relationship is an essential part of the healing.

4. No Labels

Unlike mainstream medicine, which relies on *the label* to determine the treatment, functional medicine practices repair without a label. It seeks to heal the child's learning, behavior or mood symptoms by finding and fixing what's not working in your child's body. A customized treatment plan can typically include some of the following: anti-fungals, supplements to correct vitamin and mineral deficiencies, heavy metal detoxification, specialized diet and exercise, botanical medicines, psychotherapy or other specialized therapies, and NeuroParenting. When correctly applied, the customized treatment will restore the spirit-body-brain balance and the troublesome learning, behavior and mood symptoms your child has been grappling with will disappear – or be significantly reduced.

What is so unique about the functional approach is that without needing a label for diagnosis or treatment purposes, it provides:

1. A method for identifying the chain of breakdowns in the body and brain.

2. A method for repairing and rebalancing the biomedical and neurochemical systems.
3. A method for addressing lifestyle issues that contribute to the internal malfunctions.

When this repair work is completed, the body's natural healing forces take over.

Labels Are Dangerous.

Soren Kierkegaard, the Danish philosopher, poet and social critic said: "When you label me you negate me."

Labels stigmatize us. In fact, I believe that labeling a child is a criminal act. Think about it. The minute your child has been diagnosed with a label, the way you perceive your child is tainted forever! Never again will you be able to see the perfect beauty of the child without thinking about the label the child now carries. Forever more, you will behave in response to your child in accordance with the label that has been placed on them... unless you are a very rare human being. I have seen the power of labels to make or break, destroy or build, enhance or diminish ourselves and others. Think about the enormous impact a positive or negative label can have on a child when uttered by a teacher. Think about the labels that doctors and psychiatrists place on their patients.

As adults we have the ability to intellectually and emotionally reject a label that someone has placed on us, and even then, it is really difficult to do because it keeps ringing in our ears. Children don't have the

From Treating Symptoms to Treating Causes

capacity to reject diagnostic labels placed on them. As far as the child knows, this label is the truth, especially when it comes from a person "who knows." The child doesn't know that these diagnostic labels are often based on subjective evaluation or outdated information. The child doesn't know to wonder whether the label may be an unfounded perception or projection of another person.

> **Today's healthcare practitioners, teachers and parents are far too label-happy.**

If a child is rebellious, he or she gets labeled as having an oppositional defiant disorder. If your kid acts like a kid, he is labeled "ADHD." If they are sad and unhappy, they are a "depressive." Shy children can even be labeled as having a "social anxiety disorder." The diagnosis becomes part of your child's medical record. It follows them around as they grow into adulthood, despite the fact that medical evidence to prove the diagnosis is correct is often lacking.

Diagnostic labels tell the child a story about himself that sounds something like, "There is something really wrong with me. My brain doesn't work the way it should. I am not okay like other kids. I can't learn and behave in ways that others kids can. I am a problem to the teacher and my parents and even to other kids." The saddest part is that this label becomes a self-fulfilling prophecy. Children will believe *they can't*, so they can't and then they use their diagnosis as an excuse for poor performance and behavior. Teachers tell me that some kids come to school in the morning and announce to the teacher, "I can't learn today, I didn't take my medication."

A serious concern is that some teachers are diagnosing their students – "I think Peter has ADHD. You should have him tested." This is totally unacceptable. I recommend that if you have this experience with your child's teacher or with the school, you unequivocally shut them down and forbid them to mention any diagnosis in front of your child. In Section Three, chapter 11, you will read about an important parenting tool you can use to avoid labels.

Healing kids by treating the body as one system and looking for the root cause seems quite logical, doesn't it? Why isn't it happening as the standard way of treating kids? Why are parents going from one healthcare practitioner to another, looking for answers and hoping to find the magic treatment that will truly remove their child's symptoms?

Medical Specialization Was Once a Good Idea
The practice of medical specialization began in the early 19th century, and continues to this day. It was considered to be a good idea because the theory was that the body is a collection of different, separately-functioning parts. Therefore, it made sense to compartmentalize medicine and train doctors to become specialists in the treatment of these different parts. Pharmacological research followed suit, developing drugs to treat the malfunctions in the different areas of the body. As happens with all once-good ideas, compartmentalized medicine has now outlived its usefulness. It is, in fact, not only becoming redundant but is also extraordinarily limiting in its ability to create health and wellness.

I have seen how parents spend a great deal of time, money and effort putting different kinds of compartmentalized, disconnected treatment plans into practice, either at the same time, or at different times, and often nothing seems to work. Eventually, the parents and the children begin to believe that they will be stuck with the problem for the rest of their lives. Imagine, instead, being able to see one – or two

– healthcare practitioners, *working as a team*, a team that knows how to go to the root of the problem, fix it and permanently remove the learning, behavior and mood symptoms!

The Trap of Compartmentalized Medicine

What is happening:

- You are concerned about some problems your child is displaying. You visit the general practitioner. If he has the expertise to deal with these symptoms, he will treat them. If not, he will refer you to a practitioner who specializes in diagnosing and treating that kind of problem.

- You visit the specialist and hear a diagnosis, which is, in some strange way, a relief. Your inner voice exclaims, "Phew, I have a diagnosis! Finally I know what's wrong with my child." The problem is that each specialist diagnoses the child through the narrow lens of the specialist degree on his/her wall. In essence, each time they see a new patient, they ask themselves, "When I look at this child *through the lenses of my specialization*, what is the diagnostic label I can apply to this child?" If the child has chronic headaches, a psychiatrist, neurologist, psychologist, endocrinologist or nutritionist will each give you a different diagnosis and a different treatment plan for the headaches. This tunnel vision sounds like the story of the man who lost his car keys and was searching for them under a lamppost? When his friend asked, "Where exactly did you drop the keys?" the man pointed to the sidewalk across the street. "Then why on earth are you looking for them over here?" the friend asked. "Because the light is better here," he replied. Medical specialists are often looking in the wrong places, because that is where they have been trained to look.

- The practitioner prescribes medication. If your child is among the fortunate ones, the medication does not cause side effects. If you are not so fortunate, the medicine can cause all kinds of negative side effects. You will then either get an additional prescription to help deal with unpleasant side effects or be advised to try a different medication.

- If your child develops new, additional symptoms (tics, eczema, asthma, headaches, depression, irritability, tummy aches, sleeplessness…), you repeat the first three steps. You may need to visit a different kind of healthcare specialist for each new problem. Your child now has several diagnoses and several medications. But nobody is connecting the dots! Most often nobody thinks to ask, *What is the commonality among all these conditions? Could there be a common underlying root cause?* Instead, each healthcare specialist thinks they've got *the* answer. Your child could, for example, have undetected high levels of fungus in his intestines, which can explain his irritability, poor memory, headaches, emotional or behavior problems. You would be surprised how differently children feel and behave when the fungus is removed. But the compartmentalized practitioner does not even consider the possibility of fungus being a possible causative factor.

It took five years before David's mother found a healthcare practitioner who knew where to look for David's problems. The different medical specialists he visited over the years

Does the healthcare professional treating your child know how to "see the whole child?" Or is he or she practicing compartmentalized medicine?

each looked at David through the limited lens of their particular area of specialization. As the saying goes, "When you have only a hammer, everything looks like a nail." As a result, they did not discover the real source of David's problems, which continued to wreak havoc on David's body, brain and spirit. Imagine the anguish, pain, stress and sadness that David and his family would have been spared had they discovered these underlying causes when he was age six, rather than age eleven.

Your Child Does Not Have To Be a Statistic in This Epidemic

Are you excited to know that exceptional results are being achieved by finding and treating the root causes? Are you eager to Take Charge and start the process of discovering what is really happening to your child?

Read on and learn:
1. If your beliefs are holding you back.
2. About the *Parents, Take Charge* Program.
3. What kind of possible root causes you could be looking for.
4. Who can help you find these answers.

CHAPTER 4
Are Your Beliefs Keeping You Stuck?

I Packed Your Parachute

After 75 combat missions, his plane was destroyed by a surface-to-air missile. Plumb ejected and parachuted into enemy hands. He was captured and spent six years in a communist Vietnamese prison. He survived the ordeal and now lectures on lessons learned from that experience!

One day, when Plumb and his wife were sitting in a restaurant, a man at another table came up and declared, "You're Plumb! You flew jet fighters in Vietnam from the aircraft carrier Kitty Hawk. You were shot down!"

"How in the world did you know that?" asked Plumb.

"I packed your parachute," the man replied. Plumb gasped in surprise and gratitude. The man pumped his hand and said, "I guess it worked!"

Plumb assured him, "It sure did. If your chute hadn't worked, I wouldn't be here today."

Plumb couldn't sleep that night, thinking about that man. He says, "I kept wondering what he had looked like in a Navy uniform: a white hat, a bib in the back and bell-bottom trousers. I wonder how many times I might have seen him and not even said, 'Good morning, how are you?' or anything, because, you see, I was a fighter pilot and he was just a sailor." Plumb thought of the many hours the sailor had spent at a long wooden table in the bowels of the ship, carefully weaving the shrouds and folding the silks of each chute, holding in his hands, each time, the fate of someone he didn't know.

Sometimes in the daily challenges that life gives us, we miss what is really important. We may fail to say hello, please, or thank you, congratulate someone on something wonderful that has happened to them, give a compliment, or just do something nice for no reason. As you go through this week, this month, this year, recognize people who pack your parachutes.

Thank you for your part in packing my parachute by reading this book. Don't forget to thank those who have helped pack yours!

Are you ready to pack your child's parachute?

Update Your Beliefs.

Taking Charge begins by first understanding your personal belief system, which is vitally important because our beliefs drive our behaviors. If we have outdated beliefs, we will behave in outdated ways that are unlikely to bring positive outcomes. Functional medicine challenges many of the beliefs surrounding traditional medicine. Before you adopt this new option and start this journey, it is an important first step to be sure there is a good fit between what you believe and the fundamental beliefs of this approach.

Any healthcare practitioner using an approach that fails to help children overcome their problems can only continue to practice in this way because they are supported by parents who hold onto outdated beliefs that are no longer appropriate for the 21st century. Now is a good time to do a spring-cleaning of your beliefs regarding your child's challenges.

PARENTS, TAKE CHARGE!

Check your beliefs against these below and, if necessary, consider updating those that are outdated. The outdated belief is written on the top line. The updated belief starts on the second line.

1. **The doctor knows best.**
No, not always and not all doctors. The best combination is a doctor who listens to the wise and wonderful intuition of the mom and dad.

2. **If I have a diagnosis, I will know what is wrong with the child.**
No, you won't because the diagnosis will not tell you why the child has these problems. If you don't know why, you can't remove the problem, you can only suppress it, or manage it, or control it with medication.

3. **If it is a learning, behavior or mood problem, it is probably a brain disorder.**
No, it isn't! It is most likely some problem in the child's spirit and body that is affecting the brain's ability to function correctly.

4. **Medication will cure the problem.**
No, it won't. It will only mask the symptoms. The cause of the problem will remain undetected and untreated. Eventually, this undetected underlying root cause will even interfere with the ability of the medication to suppress the symptoms.

5. **I can ignore the role played by stress.**
No, you can't ignore stress. Ignoring stress is what triggered the problems in the first place. If you continue to avoid facing the stress factors, existing symptoms will become worse and new ones can develop.

6. **The child's genes are the cause of the problems.**
No, they don't have to be the cause. This belief is an old-fash-

ioned idea. We can switch our genes on or off with the food we eat, the lifestyle we live, the relationships we have, the exercise we do and the way we behave.

7. **My child inherited these problems.**

No, he cannot inherit learning, behavior or mood problems. These are not diseases, they are symptoms of stress. Children copy Mom or Dad's stress behavior patterns which can then trigger learning, behavior or mood problems. We refer to this as intergenerational transmission of behavioral patterns.

How Did You Match Up?

If you agree with the updated beliefs, then you are already a step ahead. Or perhaps you have been inspired to discard your old beliefs and update your beliefs with these. Congratulations – you have taken the first step. If you are unable to agree with one or more beliefs mentioned above, take note of the differences and read further. The information you learn may shift your beliefs.

The story at the beginning of this chapter describes how Charles Plumb, a US Navy jet pilot in Vietnam, met the man who had packed the parachute that saved him when he ejected after his plane was shot down by a surface-to-air missile. Plumb described the immense gratitude he felt for this man. Today, he inspires audiences with his story and asks them to think about and thank the people in their lives who "pack their parachute."

One of the most profound things you can do for your children is to *pack their parachute*. When you understand how to discover and fix what is causing your child's symptoms, you are parachuting them out of a life filled with continual struggle into a life of joy and well-being.

PARENTS, TAKE CHARGE!

Are you ready to pack your child's parachute?

Now let's learn about the *Parents, Take Charge* Program.

CHAPTER 5
About the *Parents, Take Charge* Program

When Kids Speak With Their Spirit

A small boy is sent to bed by his father. Five minutes later… "Da-ad…"

"What?"

"I'm thirsty. Can you bring me a drink of water?"

"No. You had your chance. Lights out."

Five minutes later… "Da-aaaad….."

"WHAT?"

"I'm THIRSTY. Can I have a drink of water??"

"I told you NO! If you ask again, I'll have to spank you!!"

Five minutes later… "Daaaa-aaaad…"

"WHAT!"

"When you come in to spank me, can you bring a drink of water?"

An exasperated mother, whose son was always getting into mischief, finally asked him, "How do you expect to get into Heaven?"

The boy thought it over and said, "Well, I'll run in and out and in and out and keep slamming the door until St. Peter says, 'For Heaven's sake, Dylan, come in or stay out!'"

One summer evening during a violent thunderstorm, a mother was tucking her son into bed. She was about to turn off the light when he asked with a tremor in his voice, "Mommy, will you sleep with me tonight?"

The mother smiled and gave him a reassuring hug. "I can't dear," she said. "I have to sleep in Daddy's room."

A long silence was broken at last by his shaky little voice: "The big sissy!"

A kindergarten pupil told his teacher he'd found a dead cat.

"How do you know it was dead?" she asked her pupil.

"Because I pissed in its ear and it didn't move," answered the child innocently.

"You did WHAT?!?" the teacher exclaimed in surprise.

"You know," explained the boy, "I leaned over and went Pssst! in its ear and it didn't move."

Have you noticed how your child's feisty and funny spirit reveals itself?
Have you felt the blessing of this?

A Liberating Experience for Parents

In the previous chapter we read that Functional Practitioners are able to treat the body and brain as ONE integrated system because they understand how every organ and biological system are connected to each other, and how they depend on each other to function effectively. To discover where functional breakdowns may have occurred, practitioners obtain a comprehensive patient history. The child's story will give them the clues about what could have gone wrong. The practitioner then calls for tests to verify this.

Having a skilled practitioner diagnose and treat the body and brain as ONE can be *a huge relief for parents*, who may have been going from one specialist to another, without anyone connecting the dots. No more confusing diagnoses, such as: the neurologist diagnosing the child's depression as a brain disorder, the psychologist identifying it as an emotional disorder, and the nutritionist relating it to a food allergy. The end of each practitioner believing that he or she has the right answer, but, like the blind men and the elephant, they don't because they are not seeing the whole child. No more stigmatizing labels of: ADD, OCD, ADHD, ODD, and depression. Instead, just the identification of some interrelated body-brain malfunctions that can be repaired.

There is still one piece missing.

The *Parents, Take Charge* Program

The *Parents, Take Charge* Program takes the concept of ONE body-brain system to another level by including yet another missing piece – *the spirit*. *Parents, Take Charge* is based on the principle that the role of spirit is pivotal in causing and healing learning, behavior and mood problems.

Since *spirit* is such a fundamental part of the *Parents, Take Charge* Program let's be sure that we all interpret what this word means in the same way.

Our *spirit* is the very personal essence of our being. It is the core of who we are and how we live in the world. Webster and others define spirit as:

- Our life force
- That which gives life to the physical organism
- The breath of life – derived from the Latin word *spiritus*, for breath
- The animating or vital principle
- A mood or emotional state that defines us

Note that the term spirit has no necessary connection to religion. Spirit may find a mode of expression through formal religion but spirit exists with or without religion.

My favorite definition is that *our spirit is our life force*. And when our life force is alive and well, we are alive and well.

It All Begins With Spirit

Fundamental to the *Parents, Take Charge* Program is that a healthy spirit is the necessary foundation for the effective functioning of the body-brain and that all body-brain imbalances begin with an unhappy spirit. A happy spirit equals a happy body and a happy brain. When spirit-body-brain lose the natural ability to "dance together" in harmony, learning is impacted, feeling good does not come naturally and behavior becomes dysfunctional. When these three aspects of the child's being, spirit-body-brain, have lost the natural ability to "dance together" in harmony, learning is impacted, feeling good does not come naturally and behavior becomes dysfunctional. The goal of the *Parents, Take Charge* Program is to restore the natural ability of the spirit-body-brain to "dance together."

To Fix the Body and Brain We Need to Fix the Spirit.
Medicating the body and brain will not fix the spirit. It will not heal our 'life force' and when our life force is weak, we are not well. Fixing the spirit is key to fixing the body and brain, which then nourishes the spirit, which then nourishes the body and brain… This becomes a powerful circular feedback loop. In the more elaborate words of Liu Zhou, a 6th century philosopher, "If the spirit is at peace, the heart is in harmony; when the heart is in harmony, the body is whole; if the spirit becomes aggravated the heart wavers, and when the heart wavers the body becomes injured; if one seeks to heal the physical body, therefore, one needs to regulate the spirit first."

When a child's spirit is strong he feels safe in his world. When the spirit is weak the child will feel lost and unsafe. (More about this in chapter 7). A strong, healthy spirit also gives the child a deep inner sense of "I am me," which means they are connected to their true self at the core of their being. Spirited children are able to hold their self in high esteem. In other words, having a strong spirit enables them to have strong self-esteem and to know, honor, respect, value, prize and celebrate who they are. They also find it easy to respect and esteem others.

A healthy spirit impacts the way in which the child interprets events, the degree to which they take control over their own destiny, the decisions they make, their ability to be creative, to learn, to dream dreams of greatness and act upon them and the ability to give and receive love. Being connected to a healthy spirit is the foundation for happiness, success, integrity, empathy, creativity, respect, accountability, perseverance and emotional resilience. The health of the child's spirit plays a key role in determining whether he or she will fulfill their innate potential, become everything they are capable of being and live life to the fullest.

Parents, Take Charge is Based on Three Primary Principles:

1. Spirit-body-brain function as ONE interconnected system that is designed to work in complete synchronization.
2. A hurting spirit triggers a hurting body and brain.
3. The chain of interconnected spirit-body brain imbalance can trigger learning, behavior and mood symptoms.

The overarching rule of *Parents, Take Charge* is:

> The "magic" that provides the power and energy for every single life-enhancing act and thought, is our spirit - our life force.

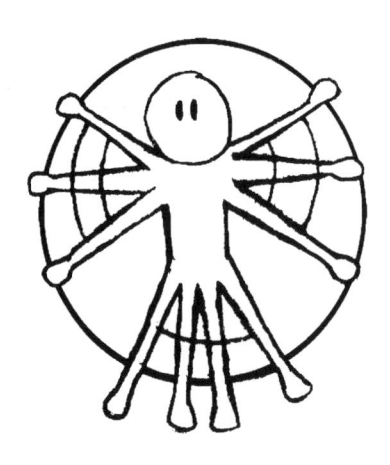

Think ONE. Diagnose as ONE. Treat as ONE.

Treating the spirit with medication or therapy, without treating the body-brain or the other way around, will not bring the desired result because the whole child is not being treated. The *spirit, body and brain need to be treated simultaneously*. Healthcare practitioners should know how to identify the pathway of psychological (spirit), biomedical (body) and neurochemical (brain) breakdowns that have occurred in the child. Repairing each of these interrelated breakdowns will restore the spirit-body-brain balance and remove the learning, behavior and mood symptoms.

Chronic Emotional Stress → **High Cortisol** → **Systemic Inflammation** → **Immune System Compromise** → **Fungus in Intestines** → **B Vitamin Deficiencies** → **Imbalanced Brain Neurochemistry** → **Hyperactivity/Impulsivity/Inattention/Temper Tantrums**

For example, a spirit-body-brain (psychological-biomedical-neurochemical) misfiring pathway could be:

In this example, the chronic stress, felt in the child's spirit, is the source of the web-like chain of malfunctions shown in the diagram above, all of which must be treated as part of an integrated treatment solution. Treating the intestinal fungus or B vitamin deficiency, without treating the hurting spirit, can have a positive effect on the child's health, learning and behavior, but the untreated stress in the child's spirit can undo this. Leaving any of the spirit-body-brain elements out of the diagnosis and treatment will reduce the probability of a successful long-term treatment outcome.

Think of how a butterfly comes into being. It starts as a caterpillar, then goes through a metamorphosis of several natural stages and emerges as a beautiful butterfly. If any of the stages of the metamorphosis do not occur, there will be no butterfly. It is the same treating children with learning, behavior and mood challenges. Each child has the inherent and natural ability to emerge as a magnificent butterfly: whole, healthy and well. The healing process must include spirit-body-brain rebalancing and rebooting and should take place in the correct order. The *Parents, Take Charge* Program provides the step-by-step process for doing this.

Parents, Take Charge is an integration of the latest research and information in functional medicine, neuroscience, interpersonal neurobiology and psychology, which is combined to form a comprehensive

3-Step Program:

FIND IT	FIX IT	FIRE IT UP

When you take your child through the three steps of the *Parents, Take Charge* Program, you will watch as the metamorphosis starts. As the biochemistry slowly comes back into balance, you will begin to see your child *shift from being dis-spirited to being spirited!*

You will notice how the spirit, body and brain begin to work in tandem with each other. A positive feedback loop starts to happen: the healthy spirit supports a healthy body and brain, which then loops back to support and build the spirit, which supports and builds the body and brain.

Not all children need to go through this metamorphosis. Some seem to be born spirited. Others, for reasons we will discuss in the next two chapters, seem to have a more sensitive and hurting spirit. Parents often wrongly interpret the behavior as part of the child's nature, "This is just the way he is. He is a sensitive child." If a child's sensitivity causes the child emotional pain, then it is not a natural part of who he is. This kind of hypersensitivity is unnatural and can be fixed.

Naturally spirited children can be sensitive too, but this trait is more about healthy sensitivity towards others. Naturally spirited children have some characteristics that hypersensitive kids often don't have. They display courage, chutzpah, determination and resilience in the face of pressure. They feel personal pride, are comfortable in their own skin, relate easily to others and find life exciting. Spirited children reach for great goals. They have the ability to use their talents to the fullest and be who they truly are at the very core of their being. Children with a stressed and hurting spirit have the potential to build a strong, resilient spirit but they cannot actualize this potential until the chemistry that supports such spirited behavior is corrected. The *Parents, Take Charge* program shows parents how to use a combination of medicine, psychology and neuroscience to help children with learning, behavior and mood problems become the spirited, healthy children they are capable of being.

What *Take Charge* Parents Will Need

Does finding and treating the underlying cause require extraordinary commitment from parents? You bet it does!

You will need:

- To never let yourself believe your child has an unsolvable problem.
- The courage of your convictions and the chutzpah to demand answers to the question, "Why is this happening to my child?"
- The strength to keep searching for the right healthcare practitioners who will FIND IT, FIX IT and FIRE IT UP.
- To invest time in learning and reading, go to workshops and lectures, and arm yourself with the latest knowledge and information.
- To be determined enough to be the child's advocate with the schools, the teachers, healthcare practitioners, and the many skeptical others who want you to medicate the problem away.
- To have the resilience to never give up, no matter how slow it may seem, or how long it may take.

Above all, being *Take Charge* parents requires that Mom and Dad have strong, healthy and happy spirits of their own! Parents with hurting spirits will struggle to heal their children. With a powerful, healthy, feisty, go-getting spirit, you will find the courage, determination, chutzpah, drive and commitment you will need to turn your child's life around.

Are You Ready to Take on This Challenge?

If your answer is "Yes!" then there is ONE more thing you need to know about the *Parents, Take Charge* Program. Read on to discover what this ONE more thing is.

PART II

CHAPTER 6
Step 1: What You Are Looking For

Mexican Fisherman Meets Harvard MBA

A vacationing American businessman standing on the pier of a quaint coastal fishing village in southern Mexico watched as a small boat with just one young Mexican fisherman pulled into the dock. Inside the small boat were several large Yellowfin tuna. The American complimented the Mexican on the quality of his fish.

"How long did it take you to catch them?" the American casually asked.

"Oh, a few hours," the Mexican fisherman replied.

"Why don't you stay out longer and catch more fish?" the American businessman then asked.

The Mexican warmly replied, "With these I have more than enough to support my family's needs."

The businessman became serious, "But what do you do with the rest of your time?"

Responding with a smile, the Mexican fisherman answered, "I sleep late, play with my children, watch ballgames, and take a siesta with my wife. Sometimes in the evenings I take a stroll into the village to see my friends, play the guitar, sing a few songs..."

The American businessman interrupted, "Look, I have an MBA from Harvard, and I can help you to be more profitable. You can start by fishing several hours longer every day. You can then sell the extra fish you catch. With the extra money, you can buy a bigger boat. With the additional income that larger boat will bring, you can buy a second boat, then a third one, and so on, until you have an entire fleet of fishing boats. Then you'll even be able to open your own cannery. Eventually, you could leave this tiny coastal village and move to Mexico City, or possibly even Los Angeles or New York City, where you could even further expand your enterprise."

Having never thought of such things, the Mexican fisherman asked, "But how long will all this take?"

After a rapid mental calculation, the Harvard MBA pronounced, "Probably about 15 to 20 years, maybe less if you work really hard."

"And then what, Señor?" asked the fisherman.

"Why, that's the best part!" answered the businessman with a laugh. "When the time is right, you would sell your company stock to the public and become very rich. You would make millions."

"Millions? Really? What would I do with it all?" asked the young fisherman in disbelief.

The businessman boasted, "Then you could happily retire with all the money you've made. You could move to a quaint coastal fishing village where you could sleep late, play with your grandchildren, watch ballgames, and take siesta with your wife. You could stroll to the village in the evenings where you could play the guitar and sing with your friends all you want."

Are you driven by what really matters in life –
or by meaningless stress and pressure?

What Are You Looking For?

I developed *Parents, Take Charge* as a 3-Step Program that can help parents understand exactly how to go about healing their children's learning, behavior and mood symptoms.

| FIND IT | FIX IT | FIRE IT UP |

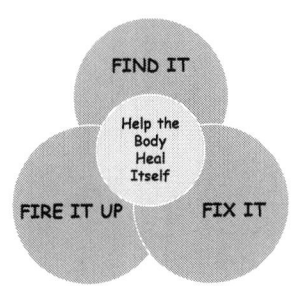

It is important to put these three steps into action in the correct sequence to ensure that your child's symptoms are eliminated. If your child is already displaying learning difficulties, inattention, hyperactivity, meltdowns, temper tantrums, anxiety, sadness, defiance, low motivation, amongst other symptoms, these are signals of a spirit-body-brain breakdown. Customarily, parents and practitioners focus on the symptoms. *What is happening? How do I make these symptoms go away?* They are putting the FIX IT step before the FIND IT step. It's like putting the cart before the horse.

The *Parents, Take Charge* way is to start an exploratory FIND IT process following the spirit-body-brain sequence that answers the following questions:

1. Why is my child's spirit hurting? Why does my child not have a strong, healthy, happy spirit?

2. How has his hurting spirit impacted his body-brain? Exactly which body-brain systems and functions have been thrown off balance by the child's hurting spirit? It's like examining faulty track lighting on the ceiling. Which lights have gone out, or are dimming? Where is the repair needed?

Once you know the answers to these questions, you can start the FIX IT and FIRE IT UP steps. Let's begin at the beginning.

Why Is My Child's Spirit Hurting?

WHY doesn't my child have a robust, resilient, confident spirit like some other children? According to the *Parents, Take Charge* approach, the answer to this question will be exactly the same for every child with any kind of learning, behavior and mood symptoms, despite the child's age or circumstances.

The answer is...

STRESS

The reasons for feeling stressed will differ from one child to another. The primary trigger for learning, behavior and mood problems is the same for every child...

STRESS

The basic beliefs of the *Parents, Take Charge* Program are that:

1. Stress is always felt in the spirit first.
2. The stressed spirit inevitably creates stress in the body-brain. Exactly which organs and systems become stressed will be different in every child. Each child's unique biological and genetic vulnerabilities will predispose them to being impacted by stress in different ways.
3. Stress sets the stage for learning, behavior and mood problems.

> Stress is like the proverbial stone thrown into a pond that creates ever increasing ripple effects.

It all Begins With Stress

With stress as the primary causative factor, the 3 steps of the *Parents, Take Charge* program are:

FIND IT	FIX IT	FIRE IT UP
FIND stress in the spirit	FIX stress in the spirit	Keep spirit FIRED UP
FIND stress in body-brain	FIX stress in body-brain	Keep body-brain FIRED UP

There is much speculation about the reason for the alarming increase in the number and severity of learning, behavior and mood problems. Certainly there are many reasons – environmental toxicity, diet, lack of exercise and lifestyle factors, being just a few. My view, based on research and my professional experience, is that the enormous stress and pressure placed on kids by society, schools and parents is a major contributor to the epidemic proportions of these problems. I consider the biochemistry of stress and the accompanying systemic inflammation to be the most dangerous and most ignored conditions in children today. (More about this in chapter 10). The chemistry associated with stress eats away at the child's spirit and throws the body and brain off balance. Unfortunately, the relationship between stress and learning, behavior and mood challenges is often not understood or it is under-diagnosed and under-estimated by healthcare providers, as well as parents.

> The staggering numbers of kids facing learning, emotional, social, behavior and health problems today is largely due to the failure to recognize stress as the primary causative factor.

The Cascading Effect of Stress

The more researchers have learned, the clearer it has become that stress may be a thread tying many symptoms together that were previously thought to be unrelated. We now know that when spirit stress is ignored and is allowed to build, it can disrupt nearly every organ system in a child's body and brain. It can disrupt the digestive system. It affects the immune, adrenal and nervous systems. When these systems are compromised, it paves the way for autoimmune disease, viral or bacterial infections, intestinal parasites, bacteria or fungus, nutritional deficiencies, hypoglycemia, vitamin and/or mineral deficiencies, sleep problems, allergies and skin conditions, amongst many other biomedical breakdowns. In the last decade, researchers have convincingly demonstrated that psychological stress can increase children's chances of developing learning, behavior and mood conditions. We have begun to understand the biomedical and neurochemical mechanisms of how this occurs.

A vicious negative cycle occurs. The stressed spirit causes biomedical problems. This dis-stresses the child even more. The increasingly stressed spirit causes more physiological irregularities, which further increases the emotional dis-stress. A vicious negative circular feedback loop is created. If the spirit and body relentlessly continue to stress each other, this will inevitably trigger neurochemical and hormonal changes that make the brain vulnerable to psychological illness, learning difficulties, anxiety, depression; and predisposes the child to an array of behavior problems, such as anti-social behaviors, violence, drug abuse or conduct disorders.

Medication can often help to manage the different spirit-body-brain symptoms. The problem is that this may require several different medications and still the primary cause remains untreated – *the child's spirit continues to feel stressed*. The medication may control the symptoms but the continuing stress can create new and additional symptoms of all kinds. As long as the emotional stress continues, the child's symptoms cannot heal. There is also the fact that medications interfere with the body's natural ability to use its own resources to self-repair, so no real healing can take place.

How Stress Works
To a parent, stress is often an emotionally loaded and misunderstood word. Before I describe the three steps of the program, I will provide you with some important facts about stress. I believe it is easier to FIND and FIX something when you have the knowledge of what is normal and healthy, and what is abnormal and unhealthy. Be aware that what I describe below, and throughout the book, applies equally to yourself as well as your children.

Not All Stress is Bad
To begin with, we should know that not all stress is bad. We need stress to survive but there is a great difference between normal levels of stress versus continually high stress levels. As an example of normal stress, imagine that you are faced with a situation that is stressful for you. It could be everyday stress like having to rush to a meeting because you are late, or driving in heavy traffic in the pouring rain. It could be emotional stress such as taking a test or having an argument with someone, or it could be real physical danger like seeing a snake in the grass. In all these situations you will feel some degree of fear. This fear triggers a chain of physiological responses known as *Fight or Flight*. The hypothalamus (H), the pituitary gland (P) and the adrenal glands (A) start sending rapid messages to each other that you perceive danger and feel fear. These three systems, known as the HPA axis, work together sending chemical messages back and forth that connect

the central nervous system, endocrine and immune systems. Your body then automatically makes several physiological changes that will give you the physical and emotional strength you will need to face the threat or to run from it. In a split-second the entire body is prepared for fight or flight. Now you can run from the snake, be extra alert in the traffic, or confront your boss.

The physiological response of fight or flight is what gives you the courage to do what needs to be done in response to a stressful situation. Think about a time when your body went into fight or flight. Perhaps you saw that you were about to have an accident or your boss began to tell you that you were fired or you confronted someone you were afraid of. Do you remember how your heart was pounding, how you were sweating, breathing heavily, how your mind and body were racing, how your muscles tightened, how all your senses were on high alert and how you broke into a cold sweat? Do you remember how, as soon as the danger passed, you returned to normal, breathing a sigh of relief?

A vitally important part of this amazing natural process is that when the danger is over or the threat has passed, these three systems (the HPA axis) start a reverse course of action to return our spirit-body-brain to a state of calm. If we do not return to a state of calm, and instead stay in a state of alarm, *this outcome becomes chronic stress.*

How Good Stress Becomes Chronic Stress

Cortisol, also known as the stress hormone, is produced by the adrenal glands. It is essential to the health and quality of our lives. You just read that in moderate amounts stress can be most beneficial. Small increases of cortisol, when needed, gives kids feelings of excitement, motivation, enthusiasm, inspiration and courage. It also helps them remain alert, be resilient and gives them the energy to rise to the challenges they face. In the case of good stress, increased cortisol is an important and helpful part of the spirit-body-brain response. It is always a short-term response because when the stressful event is over, *the cortisol levels return to normal.*

Bad stress happens when the child feels continuously emotionally overwhelmed by the demands of the outside world. Many sensitive kids are stressed around the clock, no matter whether the stress is routine or unexpected, physical or emotional, perceived or real. Their adrenal glands are on continuous "high alert," resulting in constantly high levels of cortisol that do not have a chance to return to normal because everything feels threatening to these children. The chronic fear and anxiety of these children is actually triggered by their negative thoughts, imaginations, feelings and beliefs.

> **Never underestimate the toxic stress caused by perceived threats and negative thoughts.**

They are stressed by everyday events they interpret or perceive as being threatening to their sense of well-being. Although they are not in real danger, the damaging effect of these imagined threats on the spirit-body-brain is exactly the same as if there were a real reason to feel unsafe.

Cortisol secreted for prolonged periods of time can wreak havoc on the child's physical and emotional health. The high cortisol level tricks the brain into thinking there is an emergency. But there is no real emergency, so there is too much cortisol in relation to the amount that is really needed. The continuously high levels of cortisol in the child's bloodstream can create blood sugar imbalance, suppress thyroid function and shrink the brain, amongst a long list of other possible spirit-body-brain malfunctions.

Renowned psychologist T. Berry Brazelton writes:

"Stress in small amounts is like sunshine – a little bit is fine. But, just like too much sunshine damages the skin, too much stress damages the brain.... With small amounts of stress one can learn the tools to adapt to it; however, children in our society today are dealing with insurmountable amounts of stress on a daily basis. This abundance of perpetual stress... is responsible for the marked increase of psychological disorders in children."

Do You Recognize Your Child's Stress Signals?

Research studies show that childhood stress is escalating and that parents can sometimes be unaware of the degree to which stress is affecting their children. The American Psychological Association's comprehensive study, "Stress in America," conducted in 2009, published in 2010, revealed a finding that parents grossly underestimate the extent of their child's stress. This lack of awareness of stress in kids is often encouraged by traditional doctors who ignore the role played by stress and focus instead on treating the child's external symptoms with prescription drugs. The most damaging and unfortunate part of this problem is that stress is not recognized as being a major contributing factor in the child's symptoms, so nobody addresses it, which means no true healing can take place.

Each child responds to stress differently. You are your child's stress detective. It is important to become aware of stress signals in your child, preferably as early as possible, to avoid allowing the stress to become chronic. But it is also important not to overreact. You would only need to become concerned if you notice the same or different stress symptoms occurring more and more often. Ask yourself: How often am I seeing these symptoms? What seems to trigger these reactions? When does it occur? Does the stress involve the same persons or activities? Does it happen in certain places? Is the child overtired when it happens? Is the child hungry when it happens? What did the child eat just before the sign of stress?

If signs of stress persist, you may want to seek professional advice. Functional practitioners will help you explore different possible causes for the stress, such as: relationship factors, what's happening at school and at home, the wrong diet, environmental toxins, vitamin and mineral imbalances and deficiencies, lack of essential nutrients, lack of exercise, food allergies and other lifestyle or traumatic issues.

Some stress signals to look out for are listed below. If any of these common stress signals occur with regularity, it may be a sign of chronic stress and a hurting spirit.

Some Emotional Stress Signals – a Hurting Spirit
- Hypersensitivity
- Clinging
- Mood swings
- Achievement anxiety
- Low self-esteem and self-confidence
- Fear and anxiety about most things
- Resistance to change
- Hyper-aggression
- Defiance

- Over-submissiveness
- People pleaser
- Withdrawal or outbursts
- Major change in temperament
- Antisocial behaviors

Some Physical Stress Signs – a Hurting Body
- Frequent headaches, stomach aches
- Frequent nausea, diarrhea, constipation, stomach ache, vomiting
- Nail biting
- Shaky hands, sweaty palms, feeling shaky, lightheadedness
- Increase in allergic or asthmatic attacks
- Bedwetting
- Trouble sleeping, nightmares
- Change in appetite – eating more or eating less
- Stuttering
- Frequent colds, ear infections
- Complaints of fatigue and vague illness
- Tics
- Hyperactivity

Some Learning Stress Signals - a Hurting Brain
- Decline in academic performance
- Working much harder at school or working less

- Low attention span
- Poor memory
- Incomplete schoolwork
- Specific learning problems

It is interesting to see how some children cope well with academic, social and emotional stress and pressure, and yet others find it overwhelming. **In the next chapter you will learn why some kids can handle stress and others can't.**

My guess is that the Mexican fisherman's children wouldn't know about stress.

CHAPTER 7
Wired For Stress

It's Your Choice – Whisper or Brick?

A young and successful executive was driving too fast down a neighborhood street in his new BMW. Suddenly, a brick smashed into the BMW's side door! He slammed on the brakes, spun the car back to the spot where the brick had been thrown, jumped out of the car, grabbed the kid who was standing there and pushed him up against a parked car shouting,

"What do you think you are doing, boy? This is a new car and that brick you threw is going to cost me a lot of money!"

"Please sir, please. I'm sorry, I didn't know what else to do," pleaded the youngster. "I threw the brick because no one else would stop."

Tears were dripping down the boy's chin as he pointed around the parked car.

"It's my brother, sir," he said. "He rolled off the curb and fell out of his wheelchair and I can't lift him up."

Sobbing, the boy asked the executive, "Would you please help me get him back into his wheelchair, sir? He's hurt and he's too heavy for me."

The driver tried to swallow the swelling lump in his throat and hold back his tears. He ran to the young man, lifted him back into the wheelchair, and checked to see that he was okay.

"Thank you, thank you," the grateful child said to him.

The man watched as the little boy walked off pushing his brother down the sidewalk. It was a long walk back to his BMW...a long, slow walk.

He never did repair the side door. He kept the dent to remind him not to go through life so fast that someone has to throw a brick at you to get your attention.

God whispers in your soul and speaks to your heart. Sometimes when you don't have time to listen, He has to throw a brick at you.

Are you listening to the whisper or waiting for the brick?

Why Would My Child Feel Stressed?

It is not uncommon for a parent to experience dismay, or even guilt, when I explain that their child's symptoms are related to stress. "Why should our child feel stress? We love and cherish her – we look after her well - she is always safe and comfortable - we give her nearly everything she wants. We are a happy couple and we are a happy family. Why then would she feel stress?"

There is no point in being surprised if you discover that your child is experiencing life as stressful. We can never know exactly what goes on in our child's spirit. If a child is sensitive and interprets his environment, people or events as being emotionally stressful, this stress feels real for that child. Every child has their own personal family and school circumstances that may be triggering a hurting spirit. There are challenges in all families and in all parent-child or sibling relationships. There are no perfect schools, teachers or friends. Children who have resilient spirits will not feel stressed by these challenges. Yet, the same family, school or social situations can be a source of much stress for a child with a more sensitive spirit.

Each child responds to their world in uniquely different ways and what may feel stressful to one child, may feel perfectly okay to another child. Why?

It has to do with whether the child's spirit feels safe or unsafe.

Some Children Feel Emotionally Safe

Some children have a calm spirit, which means their nervous system will be calm and their neurochemistry balanced. Their healthy spirit enables them to respond to life in a positive way. They do not struggle with life. They feel okay about the way their physical and emotional needs are being met; they feel okay about who they are and they feel recognized and appreciated by significant others in their life. They respond energetically and confidently to any pressures and expectations placed on them. They can handle pressure because they are adaptable and can easily go with the flow. These children will go to sleep at night with a calm and peaceful mind, looking forward to the challenges of the next day. When they become stressed, it will be short-term stress, which gives them the energy to overcome what they are dealing with, after which their stress levels return to baseline.

> When a child's spirit is calm and feels safe, his ability to learn and process information from his environment increases dramatically. He performs better academically and has an optimistic attitude.

Some Children Feel Emotionally Unsafe

There are children who have a sensitive spirit and who feel afraid and emotionally unsafe most of the time. These kids have a continuously aroused nervous system. They are in a state of constant fight or flight, which interferes with the ability to learn, feel good and behave in constructive ways. They are hypersensitive. They tend to see everything that happens as a possible threat to their happiness and well-being. Fear and anxiety becomes the lens through which they view the world. Their fearful emotions disengage their rational mind, making their thinking unclear. Their lives become a series of dramas and perceived emergencies, and they lose the ability to relax and enjoy the moment. This child may wake up each day and go to sleep each night filled with bad feelings, ranging from anxiety, fear and low self-esteem to helplessness and even hopelessness. It is extremely difficult to get children to cultivate positive attitudes while their spirit is stuck in this state of fear. It is, therefore, critically important that parents and educators have the necessary skills to bring the child's spirit and nervous system into a state of calm. You will learn how to do this in Chapters 13 and 14.

The question is *why?* Why do so many children have such sensitive and hurting spirits? Why would some children feel emotionally unsafe, insecure and stressed a great deal of the time? Why would children who live in a, warm, loving and happy environment feel emotionally unsafe and experience stress?

Some Children are Wired for Stress

One answer is that they are "wired for stress." Another way of saying wired for stress would be to say that some kids are predisposed from birth to have a spirit that is more sensitive to stress. These children come into the world already stressed and are wired to perceive the world as being a stressful place.

The negative effect of stress on teenagers and adults has been well documented. We never, however, thought of stress affecting infants and young children. We certainly never ever considered that the fetus could feel stress. Research now reveals that stress can start in the womb and the effects of this can impact the child long after birth. In the last decade, a great deal of scientific research has shown how stress during pregnancy affects infants and children. This stress can even play a role in triggering learning, behavior and mood conditions.

How Does a Child Become Wired for Stress?
The details that follow are not meant to lay blame and certainly not to create feelings of guilt in any moms reading this book, since no mother-to-be would knowingly do anything that would stress the fetus.

It is now known that the environment in the womb is affected by the stress levels and physiological health, or lack of health, of the mother. This womb environment is extremely important because it is this environment that will shape the biology of the fetus. If the mother has a hurting spirit and experiences stress during pregnancy, the womb will become a high stress environment and this will take a toll on the fetus. Studies are now showing that although the fetus does not have the cognitive capacity to interpret something as *stressful*, it can nevertheless experience stress through the mother's chemistry, which puts the child at a higher risk for all kinds of stress-related problems later in life.

When the pregnant mother is stressed, several biological changes occur, including elevation of stress hormones. Robin Karr-Morse in the excellent book: *Scared Sick: The Role of Adult Trauma in Childhood*

Disease writes: "... variances in prenatal maternal cortisol levels appear to be a major key to variances in cortisol levels of the offspring of both animals and humans." The mother's HPA axis is a major influence on the HPA axis of the offspring. If the mother is stressed during pregnancy and her HPA axis is affected, her baby's HPA axis is likely to be affected too. The mother's hurting spirit and accompanying aroused nervous system may cause the baby's nervous system to be aroused too. In other words, if the fetus is in a biochemically stressful environment during pregnancy, the baby can be born with a hurting spirit "wired for stress." Robin Karr-Morse describes babies wired for stress rather vividly: *Too often, such babies emerge with their little fists already clenched, ready to fight for their lives in a dangerous world.* Children who are wired for stress are particularly susceptible to becoming chronically stressed.

A Belgian study followed seventy mother-infant pairs from the first trimester of pregnancy to age nine. Infants of highly anxious mothers had more difficult temperaments from thirty-six weeks gestational age and throughout the first seven months after birth. They cried more, were more physically active, and were more irritable. They also had more irregular biological functions (eating, sleeping and eliminating). At age nine, these children, especially the boys, were still more active, had a higher rate of attention deficits and were more aggressive and impulsive.

Intense early stress has also been shown to cause brains to develop in a way that is more aggressive, more emotionally labile, less able to read social cues and can cause imbalance between the left brain and right brain.

The physical well-being of the pregnant mother is very important and can also shape the biology of the fetus. A healthy diet and good supplements are critically important to ensure healthy spirit-body-brain fetal development.

Some Children Have Good Reason to Feel Unsafe.

Clearly not all children are wired for stress. Millions of children have a whole range of existential reasons to be stressed. Others have been traumatized by terrible experiences. In 1989, Marilyn Essex launched what is now called the Wisconsin Study of Families and Work. Her team has since collected an array of medical and demographic information on several hundred children from birth to early adulthood. In a study of this sample published in 2002, Essex reported that 4-year-olds exposed to high levels of everyday stress - such as maternal depression, parental arguments and financial woes - as infants and toddlers have high amounts of the stress hormone cortisol in their saliva. These high cortisol levels correlated with aggression, impulsivity and other behavioral problems when the children were observed two years later.

Millions of children around the globe live in toxic and dangerous environments. They have very real reason to be afraid. They may be surrounded by gangs, and witnesses to crime and violence. They need to be constantly vigilant and are always afraid they will become the next victim. Children that have alcoholic, violent and incompetent parents will be in a constant state of fear and anxiety. Poverty also creates enormous stress and pressure. Can you begin to imagine the chronic stress that children living in such circumstances must feel? Their spirits are screaming with fear. Being in continuous fight or flight is a survival mechanism for them but this will have hugely negative effects on their spirit-body-brain health.

Bad News and Good News!

The bad news: whether in the womb or later in life, stress is contributing to a dramatic increase in autoimmune disease, anxiety, depression, bipolar disorder, obsessive compulsive disorder (OCD), attention deficit hyperactivity disorder (ADHD), conditions on the autism spectrum - to name just a few - in children of all ages.

The good news: if you believe your child may be wired for stress, or is finding life stressful, the good news is there's a great deal you can do that will rewire the child to be emotionally robust, with a healthy, happy spirit-body-brain. The three steps of the *Parents, Take Charge* program, as laid out in the following chapters, will show you exactly how.

Whisper or Brick?

Does your child take everything very seriously? See the worst in every situation? Feel as though he or she is unworthy and others don't like him? Does he or she take everything very personally? Can you see how much your child's spirit is hurting?

> *Dealing with your child's stress now will be far more beneficial to the child's long-term health and well-being, than spending a lifetime compensating for the damage to the spirit-body-brain that the stress has created.*

As we read in the story at the beginning of this chapter, it is better to listen to the whisper than wait for the brick.

In the previous chapters we:

- Discussed why parents should take charge
- Highlighted the difference between mainstream and functional medicine

- Introduced the basic principle of the *Parents, Take Charge* Program – the spirit-body-brain is one system
- Discovered how stress is the original trigger
- Learned that some children are wired for stress

Now let's learn how to put the *Parents Take Charge* Program into practice.

CHAPTER 8
Who Can Help You FIND IT

Lawrence Anthony (1950 - 2012)

Lawrence Anthony is a legend in South Africa. He bravely rescued wildlife and rehabilitated elephants all over the globe from human atrocities, including the courageous rescue of Baghdad Zoo animals during US invasion in 2003. He was the author of three books, including the bestseller, *The Elephant Whisperer*. On March 7, 2012, Lawrence Anthony died.

He is remembered and missed by his wife, two sons, two grandsons and numerous elephants. Two days after his passing, separate herds of wild elephants showed up at his home to say goodbye to their beloved man-friend. A total of 31 elephants had patiently walked over 12 miles to get to his South African House.

Witnessing this spectacle, humans were in awe, not only because of their supreme intelligence and the precise timing that these elephants sensed about Lawrence's passing, but also because of the profound memory and emotion the animals showed in such an organized way: walking slowly – for days – making their way in a solemn one-by-one line from their habitat to his house.

Lawrence's wife, Francoise, was especially touched, knowing that the elephants had not been to his house prior to that day for well over three years! Yet they knew where they were going. The elephants obviously wanted to pay their deep respects, honoring their friend who'd saved their

> lives – so much respect that they stayed for two days and two nights without eating anything.
>
> *Parents have a supreme intelligence and immense intuition when it comes to knowing what is hurting their children and what they need.*
>
> *Are you using yours?*

The 3-Step *Parents, Take Charge* Program:

FIND IT	FIX IT	FIRE IT UP
FIND stress in the spirit	FIX stress in the spirit	Keep spirit FIRED UP
FIND stress in body-brain	FIX stress in body-brain	Keep body-brain FIRED UP

In this chapter we will focus on: **Who can help you FIND IT?**
In the following chapters we will look at how to **Fix It** and **Fire It Up**.

Finding the Right Healthcare Team

One of the central aspects of *Parents, Take Charge* is that you, the parent, become the leader of a team of carefully selected healthcare experts who will treat your child. This is called the Core Team. Each member of the Core Team will bring their specific area of expertise to the diagnosis and treatment of the child, and together they will have the ability to explore and treat the *whole child*. As the parent, you will bring your intuition and insights. You will also form the glue for the team.

The Core Team consists of:
- The Functional Parent/s
- The Functional Psychologist
- The Functional Medical Practitioner
- The Functional Nutritionist

CORE TEAM
1. The Functional Parent/s
2. The Functional Psychologist
3. The Functional Medical Practitioner
4. The Functional Nutritionist

Each member of the Core Team should be a healthcare practitioner who applies the science of functional medicine to their field of healthcare. There could be an overlap of skills amongst the members of the Core Team, so the Core Team could consist of either two or three practitioners. In some cases, the functional medical practitioner is also well schooled in nutrition, so the Core Team will consist of two practitioners instead of three. In other cases the services of a functional nutritionist are required. Now you have a team of three, plus parents. Leaving yourselves or any of the practitioner expertise described above, out of the Core Team, will reduce the chances of real healing taking place.

The Roles of the Core Team

1. The Role of the Functional Parent

a. Parent as Communicator

In many cases, the practitioners on the Core Team are partners or associates in the same practice. In other cases, they have independent practices. It is your responsibility as a parent to ensure that if these practitioners practice independently, they are prepared to confer with each other. I highly recommend that you ask any practitioners treating your child whether they are willing to share test results, ideas, thoughts and information with each other; and whether they are prepared to do this on a regular basis. In other words, if they do not practice out of the same office, you still want them to act as an integrated team treating your child. If they are unhappy about this expectation, or if they agree, but do not follow through, they are not the right practitioners for you because they may prefer to practice compartmentalized medicine (Remember the blind men and the elephant?). Once you have the right team in place, it is your responsibility to form the glue for this communication. It's up to you to ensure that all information passes from one to the other, that you ask questions of each one, that you keep them all updated on the child's progress, and that you set up conference calls when you have a concern.

Once the treatment plan is in place and you are beginning to see results, you will need to consult with the Core Team less and less. You will know when it is time to reduce the involvement of each of the above practitioners by watching your child's progress. In the beginning, however, this Core Team will be vital to your success.

b. Parent as Partner

Most important of all, you, the parent, become an active and vitally important partner with the Core Team. After all, you are the mom or dad and you know the child better than anyone else. The intuition of a parent is extremely valuable in finding and fixing problems in their children. Practitioners working with the philosophy of functional medicine know how vital it is to listen carefully to parent insights and also to empower parents with information, tools and support. It is the parents who can make or break the success of the treatment. True functional practitioners are likely to encourage and support the idea of the parent being an active member of the team.

c. Parent as Healer

Parents play a pivotal role in healing the child's spirit-body-brain. Every word you utter, every gesture you make, every conversation you have with your child, the things you say and the things you don't say, the things you do and don't do, will either enhance their healthy chemistry or add to the stress chemistry flowing through them.

Just as you want your child's healthcare team to have functional medicine skills, you will need functional parenting skills. You cannot be a productive partner in your child's healing process if your parenting skills are not functional. It is important for parents to understand the positive and negative effect their behavior can have on their child's chemistry. Without functional parenting skills, and even with all the love in the world, you may unintentionally be obstructing or slowing down your child's healing.

There are several ways you can learn these functional parenting skills. Ideally, the functional psychologist on the Core Team will coach you in this. Or you can join one of my online classes.

In the FIRE IT UP phase of the *Parents, Take Charge* Program, I teach moms and dads, grandparents and caregivers functional parenting skills. I call this **NeuroParenting**. NeuroParenting skills empower parents to play a vital role in repairing and building their child's healthy spirit-body-brain. Using these skills is an easy and fun way of parenting that is vitally important because the child's neurochemistry is being interactively enhanced on a daily basis through his or her relationship with Mom and Dad. You will learn how to practice these skills in Part Three of the book.

2. The Role of the Functional Medical Practitioner

This member of the team will have the skills to look at the genetic make-up of the child and also investigate which biomedical and neurochemical processes in the child's spirit-body-brain are not functioning correctly. This investigation is done through extensive history taking, asking questions that most mainstream practitioners do not ask, physical examination and laboratory testing and using tests and laboratories that many mainstream doctors do not use. The functional medical practitioner may also investigate lifestyle factors, and test for allergies, food sensitivities and intolerances, heavy metal toxicity and vitamin and mineral deficiencies. Based on the results of all the tests, he or she will develop a treatment plan that will repair the identified spirit-body-brain malfunctions and result in the eradication of the child's specific learning, behavior or mood problems.

3. The Role of the Functional Nutritionist

This member of the Core Team will study the results of all the tests ordered by the functional medical practitioner, as well as the history obtained by the functional psychologist. She or he will analyze the child's diet, lifestyle, nutritional, vitamin and mineral deficiencies and take special note of any allergies and food intolerances. She will then develop a customized diet, or recommend the correct therapeutic diet, to address the child's specific problems. She may also suggest a treatment plan to help repair any identified digestive dysfunctions. This member of the Core Team also educates parents about food and supplements, about what is happening in their child's body nutritionally, as well as offering recipes and shopping strategies.

In some instances, it is okay to go directly to a skilled functional nutritionist, without first visiting the medical practitioner. These nutritionists will have the ability to order the required urine, saliva, poop, hair or blood tests to check for environmental, allergic, food sensitivity and digestive issues. Such skilled nutritionists will understand how to analyze the results and treat any malfunctions the tests reveal. Typically, working with a skilled functional nutritionist should always produce some noticeable improvement in the child's symptoms. If, however, after a good period of time, treatment does not produce enough results, then there may be other physical problems that need to be identified and a visit to the medical practitioner could become necessary.

4. The Role of the Functional Psychologist

I do not believe there is a title yet for the kind of therapist I am describing. If I could choose a title, it would be a Functional Psychologist. However, the term functional psychology has been around for a long time and is defined in a totally different way. Nevertheless, for the purposes of this book, I will use the term functional psychologist to describe this member of the Core Team. This psychologist is well read in functional medicine and interpersonal neurobiology.

In the *Parents, Take Charge* Program, the functional psychologist works with the parents as well as the child. Remember that the fundamental beliefs of *Parents, Take Charge* are that:

- Every child (and every parent) has the capability to have a healthy spirit.
- Ongoing stress impairs their spirit.

Therefore, the role of the functional psychologist is to reduce stress chemistry and free the strong, resilient spirit of the parents and their children.

PARENTS	CHILD
Goals of coaching:	**Goals of therapy:**
• To reduce stress.	• To rewire the child's brain from stress to joy.
• To FIRE UP the neurochemicals that supports a healthy spirit.	• To help the child make friends with their happy, health spirit.
• To teach NeuroParenting – the *functional parenting skills* that will FIRE UP the child's healthy neurochemistry.	• To FIRE UP the child's healthy neurochemistry.

Traditional talk therapy tends to deal with emotions and behavior in a compartmentalized way. Functional therapy, on the other hand, is spirit-body-brain therapy, dealing with the whole person. What this means is that the functional psychologist observes the behavior and emotions of the child, understands what chemistry is driving this and engages in ways that will stimulate healthy chemicals such as serotonin, endorphins, oxytocin, dopamine, and others. These are the chemicals that support awareness, love, presence, connectedness, compassion, happiness, gratitude courage and empathy. Practicing in this way, the functional psychologist deals with the underlying neurochemistry, not only the symptoms.

An excellent form of functional therapy that I would highly recommend is *Mindfulness*. Mindfulness therapists are achieving excellent results in healing spirit-body-brain problems.

The Limitations of Traditional Psychotherapy
Children who struggle with learning, behavior and mood issues are, understandably, often stressed and anxious. Their adrenal system is in overdrive, their nervous system is aroused and they spend much of their time in fight or flight. It is in this condition that they arrive for their therapy session. This physiology makes traditional talk therapy extremely difficult. The very best therapist will struggle to make a sustainable difference if the child's nervous system is on the alert and the child is in fight or flight. In this state, they cannot absorb and retain what they are hearing. Nor will traditional therapy be effective with children who have behavior problems, if these problems are being driven by undetected low levels of zinc, omega3 fats or high levels of copper, mercury and lead (amongst other examples). Expecting a child, who has low dopamine, to manage his hyperactivity with the help of traditional psychotherapy will only, at best, produce minimal, and short term results.

Brad is an example of the limitations of compartmentalized traditional psychotherapy. He is an eleven-year-old boy who was being treated by a psychologist for anxiety and irritability, being lethargic, and as his mom described it, "Just not being there." He also had abdominal pain and diarrhea. The symptoms were thought to be psychological – signs of high anxiety and depression. Therapy was marginally successful. A friend of Mom's suggested that Brad be tested for gluten intolerance. He tested positive and began a strict gluten-free diet. Within three months there was a significant improvement. He became energetic, far less irritable, fully present and engaged well with others. His happy, positive, confident spirit began to emerge. It was evident that the previously untreated gluten intolerance had played havoc with his spirit-body-brain. Therapy focused on helping Brad 'make friends' with his happy spirit. With the gluten removed from his system, the fogginess was gone from his brain and Brad could benefit from what he learned in his therapy sessions.

Practicing functional psychology does not mean that the psychologist needs to become an MD or a neurologist. The psychologist will, however, need to be educated in the fundamentals of Functional Medicine. There are excellent Functional Medicine courses available that psychologists can attend to enhance their spirit-body-brain knowledge.

The Secondary Team

Depending on the symptoms the child is grappling with, other specialized therapies are often useful to bolster the child's healing. These therapists will become your Secondary Team members (see next page).

The nature of this team will be determined by the kind of symptoms the child displays. Some children need occupational therapy; others need sensory integration therapy or perhaps speech therapy or behavior therapy, amongst others. There is a large range of excellent therapies available that can support the treatment regimen of the Core Team. The diagram below shows only a small example of possible secondary therapies.

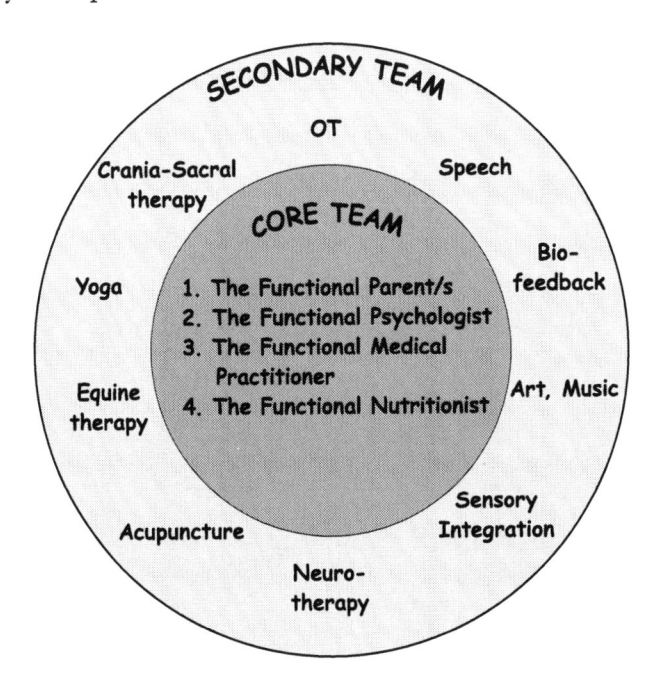

Secondary Team: OT, Speech, Bio-feedback, Art, Music, Sensory Integration, Neuro-therapy, Acupuncture, Equine therapy, Yoga, Crania-Sacral therapy

Core Team:
1. The Functional Parent/s
2. The Functional Psychologist
3. The Functional Medical Practitioner
4. The Functional Nutritionist

It is important that the use of these excellent resources occurs in the correct order in terms of the treatment process. I *highly* recommend that you first work with the Core Team before visiting any practitioners in the secondary team. You will get far better sustainable, long-term results from these therapies after first removing any identified root causes in the FIND IT phase. If you try any of these secondary therapies first, untreated root causes may interfere with the child's ability to use these therapies to best effect.

Trust Your Intuition

The touching story at the beginning of this chapter reminds us how intuitive elephants are. I would like to remind you how intuitive you are as a parent. Listen to your inner voice as you go on this journey to heal your children and trust your intuition.

In the next chapter I will introduce you to a *Parents, Take Charge* family. Reading how they put the FIND IT and FIX IT steps of *Parents, Take Charge* into practice will show you how to apply these steps to your own situation. You will also understand how and why this approach can transform children's lives and, in so doing, the lives of parents and families.

CHAPTER 9
What You May Find and How to Fix It

A Problem is a Problem

One day, the guardian of a temple dies, and the master has to replace him. The master gathered his disciples together to choose who would have the honor to work side by side with him. "I will present you all with a problem. Whoever solves it first will be the new guardian of the temple," said the master. Shortly thereafter, the master had a small coffee table brought into the center of the room. Subsequently, the master had an obviously expensive and beautiful porcelain vase, adorned with a beautiful rose, placed on the coffee table.

"This is the problem," said the master pointing at the vase and the rose it contained.

The disciples contemplated the vase, perplexed by its rare, sophisticated design, coupled with the rose's freshness and elegance.

"What did the vase symbolize? What should we do? What is the enigma?" they wondered. All the disciples stared at the vase for hours. Time passed, and no one was able to figure out what was wrong with the beautiful vase, until one of the disciples stood up. He looked at the master and the disciples, decidedly walked towards the vase, picked it up, and threw it on the floor, smashing it into hundreds of pieces. Almost in unison, all the disciples gasped, not believing what they had just witnessed.

The master got up from where he was sitting and exclaimed, "Finally, someone did it!" He looked at the disciple who had broken the vase and said, "You are the new guardian of the temple."

The master explained to the disciples: "I was very clear in pointing out the problem. You stood in front of the problem. It does not matter what the problem might be, it has to be eliminated. A problem is a problem. It could be a very expensive porcelain vase; it could be a love, who meant something at one time, and is no more, or a well-traveled road that needs to be abandoned, even though traveling through it comforts us. There is only one way to deal with a problem: take the bull by the horns. Remember that a problem is a problem. It does not make any sense to accommodate it, and look at it from different angles. It is nothing more than a problem. Do not run away from it. Deal with it. Set it aside, and continue to enjoy the beautiful things life has to offer."

Are you taking the bull by the horns?

Take the Bull by the Horns

The *Parents, Take Charge* Program shows you exactly how to do this.

FIND IT	FIX IT	FIRE IT UP

The power of this program is that:

a. It is a totally personal, customized method that any parent can put into practice.
b. There are three clear steps to follow – this is your roadmap.
c. If you don't change the order of these three steps or leave any steps out, you can transform your child's life.

We know now that although children can display many of the same symptoms, the underlying causes will be different from one child to the other. What we discover in the FIND IT step will be unique to each child – which will dictate the treatment plan of the FIX IT step. The FIRE IT UP step consists of a parenting tool box that is the same for all parents.

In this chapter, I will use a case study to demonstrate how steps 1 and 2 of the program are put into action and the kind of results you can expect. It is important to keep in mind as you read this that even though every child's situation is unique in terms of cause and effect, there is one key cause that will be common to all children with learning, behavior and mood problems – these kids all have a stressed spirit that has triggered stress in the body and brain. Exactly how this shows up in each child will be different, depending on the unique biological and genetic make-up of the child and other factors such as their lifestyle, social and emotional situation, diet, and environmental impact.

Let's Say "Hello" to the *Parents, Take Charge* Family

Greg, age seven, and Mark, age eleven, are brothers. They have loving parents and are being raised in what anyone would describe as a safe, warm and happy environment.

People who know Mark are struck by his energetic and confident spirit. He is full of beans and the joys of life. Because he engages so easily with others, his peers and even adults, gravitate towards him. Mark is a good student. He applies himself diligently to schoolwork and achieves good grades. He is crazy about sports and is a natural sportsman, excelling in basketball, which is the game he loves most.

Mark is a child who displays initiative, determination and resilience in the face of pressure. He is not fazed by the ups and downs of his ten-year-old life, always seeing the "glass as half full." For Mark, each day is interesting and exciting. As you watch him, you are aware that he is comfortable with himself and even proud of whom he is. He has a tender heart and a loving soul, which manifests in his compassion for others. Even at his youthful age, Mark displays the invaluable ability of seeing the world through his own eyes and has the inner strength to stay true to - and to defend - what he feels is right for him.

Mark's younger brother, Greg, is an extremely bright and creative child. He is especially talented in mathematics. He does not, however, find life to be as easy as Mark does. He is anxious about most things - even the smallest daily challenges can throw him off balance. This anxiety is made worse because he is pessimistic about everything that happens in his world.

Although Greg is very intelligent, his teachers complain that he is not motivated to use his talents and is capable of achieving far better grades. For Mom and Dad, getting Greg to complete his homework each day is a task that is fraught with all kinds of arguments and meltdowns.

This seven-year old is highly emotional, swinging between being sad to being angry. He is hyperactive, fidgety and impulsive. He struggles with focus and attention. If you watch this young boy, you can clearly see that his spirit is hurting. He has low self-confidence and constantly puts himself down. His anxiety about not being good enough makes it very difficult for him to make and keep friends. Recently, Greg developed eczema, which along with being overweight, made him very self-conscious and increased his sadness, isolation and self-dislike.

Greg is a picky eater. His favorite foods are all things carbohydrate and he loves cheese. He is a poor sleeper and often wakes at night because of nightmares, which adds to his general anxiety, low energy and lethargy.

PARENTS, TAKE CHARGE!

Actually, Greg seems to have always had an unhappy spirit; it has become a way of life for him and his family because they have not found a treatment solution that has helped him. They tried all kinds of therapy. For a while each of these therapies offered some improvement, but it was difficult to maintain this improvement and he would continuously slip backwards.

As you can imagine this situation has been an emotional roller coaster ride for his parents; they felt happy and hopeful when they saw some progress and then felt let down when this improvement could not be sustained. Mom, Dad and the teachers did their best to be extremely supportive and encouraging, offering Greg compliments, support and advice. But all to no avail. When Greg had a meltdown, the family would say, "Oh dear, Greg's having a bad day." And they felt stressed and helpless because they did not know how to calm him and make it a good day, a good week, a good month! A good life!

Greg's parents reached a stage when they were faced with a decision – to medicate or not to medicate. Based on a great deal of information they had gleaned, they made the decision to avoid giving Greg prescription drugs, unless absolutely necessary. This decision was not popular with his mainstream doctors, certainly not with his teachers. Even uncles, aunties and friends had a great deal to say about the situation. Greg's parents discovered they were going to need the courage of their convictions to be able to stay firm with their decision and advocate for this approach.

Mom and dad decided it was time to ask and get answers to the "Why?" questions. Why did Greg have these problems? Why were his symptoms not going away? Why, with all the best intentions in the world, were they unable to help their son? Why was he filled with anxiety and fear and sadness and anger? Why would a seven-year-old child have such a hurting spirit?

The Story of Greg's FIND IT, FIX IT Journey

The Core Team

The *Parents, Take Charge* Core Team consisted of a functional psychologist, pediatrician and nutritionist.

In the FIND IT phase we used The Spirit-Body-Brain Analysis to

FIND stress in the spirit
FIND stress in body-brain

This analysis is based on the Think ONE, Diagnose as ONE, Treat as ONE principle you read about in Chapter 5. It provides the whole picture about the whole child. With a Spirit-Body-Brain Analysis, practitioners and parents can put the pieces of the puzzle together and connect the dots to form a total picture and a total treatment plan.

Appointments were scheduled for Greg and his parents with each healthcare practitioner on the Core Team:

1. Functional Psychologist – to explore why this little boy's spirit is in such distress.
2. Functional Pediatrician – to explore why Greg has the following symptoms:

- Irritability

- Attention problems
- Hyperactivity
- Low energy, lethargy
- Poor sleep pattern
- Nightmares
- Picky eater
- Carbohydrates and dairy cravings
- Overweight
- Eczema
- Mood swings, meltdowns

Note: Be aware that although some of the symptoms that Greg has may be just like those your child has, it does not mean the underlying causes or the treatment would be the same for your child. In Functional Medicine, every child is treated as being unique.

3. Functional Nutritionist – to explore every aspect of Greg's eating patterns and nutritional lifestyle

Each member of the Core Team completed their own history taking and analysis, after which we shared this information with each other.

What did we FIND?

1. The Functional Psychologist's Findings

After spending time with Greg alone and then with his parents, I discovered that Greg had been exposed to stress starting during his time in utero and also as an infant and toddler. This fact would explain why he was wired to feel stress easily and why his spirit felt unsafe.

What I Learned from the Parents:

- Mom and Dad were experiencing relationship problems during the pregnancy, which created a great deal of stress for the pregnant mom.

- Mom did not take good care of herself during the pregnancy. She did not eat well, slept badly, did not exercise and did not support her body with essential supplements.

- There was little positive contact between Mom and Dad. For example, during the pregnancy with Mark, Dad would often lovingly touch Mom's pregnant abdomen. This kind of touch is very calming to the baby. He did not do this when Mom was carrying Greg. When pregnant with Mark, Mom practiced meditation, which is calming for the fetus. She did not do it while pregnant with Greg.

- Mom had post-partum depression and was taking anti-depressants. The effects of the drugs are stressful for the baby because they cause reduced physical, emotional and verbal engagement. (Post-partum depression is the second leading cause of language delay disorders in children. Infants who have a mom who grapples with post-partum depression can later struggle with trust, bonding, affection, love and friendship).

- Greg was a colicky baby, cried a lot, did not sleep or eat well and had frequent yeast infections.

- It was not until Greg was two years old that Mom and Dad were able to resolve their differences and build a good relationship. As little as he was, Greg witnessed and heard the marital conflicts during those years.

What I Learned from Greg:

Using various games and interventions, I was able to encourage Greg to speak spontaneously about his feelings and needs without increasing his arousal and stress. I learned that:

- He is constantly on the alert, fearing that his parents might get a divorce. Although his parents have worked through their problems and are now happy together, Greg still feels unsafe. This continual anxiety increases his stress chemistry.

- Because of the parent's strife during his formative years, Greg did not get the amount and kind of attention he needed to begin to develop a strong sense of self.

- His older brother, Mark, is a hard act to follow. Everyone loves him and praises him. He is everyone's Golden Boy. He loves his brother dearly and is very proud of him but this love is tinged with a great deal of envy which stimulates unhealthy chemistry for Greg.

- When he was five years old, his nine-year-old cousin died of leukemia. He witnessed the grief of his parents and extended family. Being the kind of child who is sensitive to emotions around him, this event had a huge impact on him. The idea of death frightens him, which would increase his stress chemistry.

- Greg's peers find it difficult to engage easily with him. He feels left out and alone.

- He has a poor self-image – thinks he is ugly (although he is a rather handsome little boy).

2. **The Pediatrician's Findings**
   Tests revealed:
   - Glutathione missing gene*
   - MTHFR gene deviation**
   - Parasites and fungus in his gut
   - Lacking in important vitamins and minerals:
   - Low levels of DHA
   - Deficient in Zinc
   - B6, B12 and folate deficiency
   - Metabolic acidosis - high acidity level
   - Low levels of dopamine and serotonin
   - Gluten intolerance
   - Sensitivity to dairy

*Glutathione is responsible for detoxifying the body of toxins and heavy metals we encounter in the environment - it is our body's most powerful antioxidant. When a body gets too burdened by heavy metals and toxins, serious health problems can emerge.

**MTHFR is a common genetic deviation. A key enzyme in the body functions at a lower than normal rate, which affects processing amino acids, the building blocks of proteins. MTHFR mutations interfere with the body's ability to absorb folic acid. People with MTHFR irregularities usually have low glutathione, which makes them more susceptible to stress and less tolerant to toxins.

The Nutritionist's Findings:

Greg's diet and eating habits are a major contributing factor to the web of emotional and physiological breakdowns. His diet consists mainly of the very foods that are bad for him - carbohydrates and dairy products. Greg's picky eating was stressful for Mom and she would often let Greg have what he craved rather than deal with the emotional meltdowns, without realizing the serious ripple effects of the gluten and dairy foods.

How did we FIX IT?

Combined FIX IT Treatment Plan for Greg

Having completed the FIND IT step, we developed a personalized spirit-body-brain treatment plan for Greg. The goal is to eventually reach the point where the body is healthy enough to take over and use its natural ability to maintain homeostasis and heal itself. Until then, however, the stressed spirit-body-brain needs outside assistance to be fixed.

The Pediatrician's FIX IT

Greg was given an anti-fungal and supplements he needed such as a probiotic, omega 3, B vitamins and folate, a balanced multivitamin, digestive enzymes, Vitamin D3 and specific Glutathione boosting supplements. He was given a liver detoxifier to help his liver remove the toxins from the body, which would help with his eczema and supplements to calm his nervous system and relax him. The pediatrician recommended that Greg exercise daily. Exercise has many well-known benefits but, as the pediatrician explained to Greg's mom and dad, in Greg's case exercise was an extremely important piece of the treatment plan. The reason for this requirement is that exercise will boost Greg's glutathione levels and thereby help him boost his immune system, improve his detoxification and enhance his body's own antioxidant defenses, which will enhance brain functioning and reduce Greg's attention problems.

The Nutritionist's FIX IT

The nutritionist developed a personalized eating and lifestyle plan for Greg based on what is happening in Greg's spirit-body-brain:

- Increase MTHFR boosting foods
- Increase glutathione boosting foods
- Exclude gluten and dairy products
- Include more alkaline foods
- Avoid inflammatory foods
- Introduce safe chemicals into the household

The nutritionist knew this new diet would be a huge change for Greg and his parents. She assisted Mom with tasty recipes and shopping for the right products. To ensure the success of the transition to the new diet, she also had sessions with Greg to teach him about why he cannot eat the way he used to, what happens when he gives his body the "wrong stuff" and what his body needs instead. Greg was included in the shopping expeditions so he could be involved and discover all about the foods that are good for him. It took some time but he eventually stopped resisting the change, enjoyed being involved in the cooking and shopping, and began to notice that he actually felt better eating this way. These results reinforced his commitment to the new diet.

Within three months, the customized diet and supplements began to make Greg feel so much better. Week by week he became a little calmer; there were fewer and fewer meltdowns, he was less anxious, had more energy and his teachers reported he was more focused and motivated. When Greg's energy level had improved, Mom and Dad found a student trainer who came to their home and exercised with Greg, building his strength and confidence to exercise on his own.

The Psychologist's FIX IT

The fact that Greg's body and brain are being repaired and are healing is excellent news. The correct diet and supplements are critically important but they will not be enough to heal his spirit. That will not happen automatically. It requires special attention. Too often I have seen parents become excited by the improvements that diet and supplements make and avoid dealing with the child's hurting spirit. This avoidance is a mistake: if the spirit-stress continues, it can start to undo or reduce the benefits of the diet and supplements. When that happens, parents mistakenly think, "This plan is not working. Perhaps we need medication."

My therapy goals for Greg were to undo the stress wiring, reverse negative thoughts and feelings and release his happy, confident spirit from its prison of fear. This would let him know the sense of aliveness and would let him recapture his inner resilience. For Greg, stress had started in the womb. Then, from the time he was born he had spent his entire young life feeling emotionally unsafe, anxious, and pessimistic. He had watched his older brother, envying his ability to be so happy and free. He had heard over and over again, from his parents and his teachers, albeit told to him in a caring way, that he was getting it wrong. He was told that he was not living up to expectations; he was not being like other kids; he should try harder; he should be different. These messages were deeply wired into his psyche, and Greg and I began the work of rewiring these old messages.

It was a joy for us all to see how Greg gradually began to feel safe enough to befriend his happy spirit and connect with the unique and special little boy he is. The kids who previously ignored him began responding positively to this new Greg, which was a great boost to his self-esteem.

In chapter 1, I wrote that *beneath the layers of learning, behavior and mood issues so many children grapple with, there is a problem-free child with a healthy body, brain and spirit.* We began to see this wonderful Greg emerging.

Look at him now!
Greg has lost weight, he is bursting with energy and motivation; he is playing his favorite sport, tennis; he has made friends, is able to focus and pay attention significantly better, and is a pleasure to be around at home. Mom and dad could actually see this transformation slowly happening, month after month, as the treatment plan began to work and each of his symptoms gradually began to dissipate and then disappear. We all watched in delight as the healthy, normal, talented little boy emerged from behind all the problems that had been covering up his true spirit.

Let's connect the dots…
   a. Stress chemistry paved the way for all Greg's symptoms. (In Greg's case the stress started in the womb; other children may experience stress later).
   b. Each and every emotional, physical and learning symptom that Greg had was inter-related. It was all ONE story.
   c. Using the Parents, Take Charge rule - Think ONE. Diagnose as ONE. Treat as ONE - Greg's healing was achieved without prescriptions drugs.

Remember Greg's brother Mark?
It seems Mark's nervous system was in a state of calm from the moment of birth on. Mom had a happy pregnancy with him. When he was born, Mom and Dad poured a huge amount of love and attention on him. Like Greg, he also lived through mom and dad's relationship struggles

and the loss of a cousin to leukemia, but he coped well. Clearly, Mark has a healthy spirit, which is why he has a feeling of well-being and is able to put himself out there and enjoy being whom he is.

The good news is that, like Mark, Greg's spirit-body-brain has also started dancing in harmony. His stress wiring is being replaced with happy wiring. However, the reversal of Greg's symptoms did not happen overnight. If you are looking for a quick-fix, magic bullet, short-term solution, this method is not the option for you. This method involved a high level of commitment, courage and determination from Greg and his mom and dad.

If You Want to *Take Charge*, Know This:

1. You need to know the power to heal your children lies with you, the parents.

2. You need to know there will be highs and lows in this journey. There will be times of sheer joy as you watch your healthy child emerge as the symptoms are reversed one by one. And then there may be times when the treatment plan does not seem to be working, times when you may have to go back to the drawing board and look for yet another undetected underlying cause that may have been missed. I describe this process like peeling the layers of an onion.

3. To achieve your dream, you will need great clarity of purpose. You will need to know exactly why you have chosen this treatment option. Because this method is such a new way of helping your children, you will need to find your voice and speak out about what you are doing and why you are doing it. You will

need to have the strength and courage to take this healing journey with your children and not listen to the naysayers.

4. You will need to read everything you can lay your hands on. Attend workshops. Network with informed others who have already accomplished this new healing or who, like you, are still finding their way.

5. You will need to stay steadfast, knowing that what you are doing is far better than immediately resorting to prescription drugs. Those drugs will be there should you need them, but if you can avoid them, what a blessing that would be!

6. You will need to know there is one thing that could cause you to stumble if you decide to take this journey: your own negative thoughts. Put your fearing, naming, blaming, shaming thoughts away and have the courage and spirit to stand proud and say, *'I can do it. I can Take CHARGE!' and free my child.*

Above all, you need to know, deep in your heart, that you are giving your child the greatest gift a parent could ever give – the gift of a healthy spirit, body and brain that are all dancing in harmony together. You are reducing the chances of them being sickly adults prone to all kinds of stress-related disorders. Instead, you are giving them the chance of living a life filled with feelings of well-being and joy.

There is no greater gift.

Step 3 Coming Up!

Now that you understand how the FIND IT and FIX IT steps of the *Parents, Take Charge* Program hang together, you are ready to learn about Step Three of the program – FIRE IT UP. This step involves NeuroParenting skills. The goal of the FIRE IT UP step is to make sure that progress made in steps 1 and 2 does not unravel. The Neuro-Parenting skills are the glue that holds it all together.

PART III

CHAPTER 10
FIRE UP the Good. Calm the Bad.

Michelangelo wrote about his statue of David, "I saw the angel in the marble; I chiseled to set it free." This chapter is about chiseling to set your child free.

> **Our *Parents, Take Charge* Family**
>
> Life is very different these days in Greg's family household. Greg looks and feels good and is so proud of himself. He is a busy, happy little boy, dealing with all the normal things an almost nine year old should be dealing with. His grades are improving each week and his teachers have all mentioned the remarkable positive change in his behavior. One teacher told Mom, "It is as though a light has been switched on in Greg."
>
> Mom has made some excellent changes to the family diet. She has made some wonderful changes in her own lifestyle, too. After FINDING and FIXING her own spirit-body-brain issues, she is now several pounds lighter and migraine-free! Mom is doing something she always wanted to do but kept putting off. She bought a professional camera, joined a photography class and has started to live her dream of becoming a professional photographer.
>
> Dad, Mom, Greg and Mark all volunteer once a month at a shelter for the underprivileged. One Sunday evening on the way home, they were discussing what a wonderful experience it is to help others. Dad expressed it perfectly when he said, "I may help feed them but volunteering helps feed my spirit.

> There is a wonderful connected energy in this family that was not there before – lots of laughter, lots of hugging and lots of positive, healing conversations.
>
> *Does this sound like your family?*

From FIND IT to FIX IT and now to FIRE IT UP

Do these changes mean that Greg, whose spirit and body were in such distress, is now stress free? Does it mean that he is totally self-confident, never feels anxious and never has a meltdown? Of course not. But these symptoms have certainly decreased considerably. He copes more and more easily in situations that previously had caused him a great deal of misery. He is clearly on his way to spirit-body-brain balance.

Having achieved these excellent results, it is important to ensure that this progress is *permanent*. If Greg would eat the wrong foods or come off his vital supplements, he could begin to lose ground and eventually he could regress. In the same way, if the happy, confident, focused, courageous, optimistic chemistry that has now been stimulated is not continually supported, the stress chemistry can take over again. Thinking positively and believing in himself is still new for Greg. This new way of being will need to be skillfully nurtured and reinforced until it becomes natural for him to be this way.

This is where Mom and Dad play a critical role on a daily basis. Using NeuroParenting skills, they can continue to build and strengthen Greg's healthy spirit and prevent stress from gaining control again.

FIRE UP the Good Chemistry. Calm the Bad.

In the previous chapter, you read that the psychologist's role in the FIX IT step is to help the child, as well as the parents, befriend their healthy spirit that had been suppressed by stress.

The psychologist's role is to bring the child up to speed with having a healthy, resilient spirit. The fact is that children who have grappled with learning, behavior and mood problems have lost time, developmentally speaking. Instead of using the years to discover and develop who they are, they were grappling with their problems. They have a developmental lag in terms of knowing and being their spirited self. The good news is that they can catch up very quickly with the right help. The functional psychologist achieves this through skillfully using the therapeutic relationship to let the child experience being spirited versus being stressed. This is achieved in two ways – by calming the stress chemistry and firing up the healthy chemistry.

Parents can also do this with NeuroParenting skills. In fact, all children, whether they have problems or not, can benefit from these parenting skills. These are skills that all parents should have. In the next chapter, you will learn about FIRING UP the good chemistry. In this chapter you learn about calming the bad.

What Are You Calming?

You will need to know about *systemic inflammation*. A vitally important aspect of stress that we have not yet discussed is that chronic stress and the accompanying high level of cortisol, go hand in hand with chronic inflammation – also known as systemic inflammation. Using NeuroParenting, you are calming the stress chemistry as well as the systemic inflammation.

Where there is stress, there is inflammation.

In the case of children with learning, mood and behavior challenges, the presence of systemic inflammation is a huge piece of their problem. It's vital that parents understand:

- What systemic inflammation is
- Where the inflammation comes from
- How parent behavior can unintentionally increase the inflammation
- How they can interact with their children in ways that will reduce the inflammation

Reducing systemic inflammation is a immensely important for the child's emotional, mental and physical well-being. Let's begin by understanding the difference between good and bad inflammation.

Good Inflammation

We all need inflammation to help us when we have some kind of infection, have broken a bone, sprained our wrist or perhaps burned ourselves on a hot stove. The body assesses the level of threat and releases pro-inflammatory compounds to assist in repairing the problem. It's our immune system's way of protecting us. When the repair has been done, the body turns the inflammatory compounds off.

These situations demonstrate good, short-term inflammation. In these situations, inflammation is our friend.

When Good Inflammation Goes Bad

Systemic inflammation is not our friend. It is bad inflammation. Richard Weinstein writes in his book, *The Stress Effect*, "Systemic inflammation means that there is a highly inflammatory chemical circulating through the bloodstream." This reaction happens when the good inflammatory response is not completely turned off and continues to stimulate pro-inflammatory immune cells even though they are not needed. When these excess immune cells are circulating in our system, we have what is called chronic or systemic inflammation. Think of systemic inflammation as a slow burning, smoldering fire that spreads through our system. It can lead to serious metabolic breakdown, with huge impact on our long-term spirit-body-brain health.

Chronic inflammation is often described as *silent inflammation* because it can be happening without you even knowing it. It is called silent because it falls below the threshold of perceived pain. That's what makes it so dangerous. You don't know you have it, so you don't take any steps to stop it. Having a constant, low-grade flow of powerful inflammatory markers in the blood stream will cause spirit-body-brain damage with time. It can smolder for years, sometimes decades, eventually erupting into various forms of serious health issues. Systemic inflammation takes a huge toll on the body's energy and resources. In his book, Clean, Dr. Alejandro Junger writes, *Inflammation is very necessary when needed so it has to be ready to be sparked into action at the right time. When it is turned on permanently, it is corrosive so it needs to be turned off immediately when the job is done.*

You are, no doubt, aware that disorders like rheumatoid arthritis, inflammatory bowel disease and eczema stem from inflammation. Systemic inflammation has now been connected to obesity, diabetes, atherosclerosis and high blood pressure, Alzheimer's, Addison's disease, osteoporosis, Parkinson's, cancer and even depression. Functional practitioners view chronic inflammation as being the root cause of all degenerative illnesses and even of biological aging.

The Stress-Inflammation-Toxin Cycle

Chronic stress sets the stage for chronic inflammation which makes the spirit-body-brain susceptible to environmental and emotional toxins. A large proportion of children with cognitive, mood and behavior issues have high levels of stress, inflammation and toxins. The negative circular chain of malfunctions looks like this:

STRESS
↓
Inflammation
↓
Toxins
↓
More Inflammation
↓
Distressed spirit
↓
Stress
↓
Inflammation
↓
Toxins
↓
Learning behavior, mood, problems

The good news is that you can short-circuit this web of interactions by shutting down each aspect of the vicious cycle causing it. When we remove the original stress triggers, cool the fire of inflammation, get rid of the toxins and reverse the oxidative stress, we can help the child begin to develop a robust emotional spirit and body-brain balance. This result would not be possible while there is stress, inflammation and toxins at play.

There are two kinds of toxicity that parents should be aware of:

Environmental Toxins

We are exposed to toxins every minute of every day in the food we eat, the air we breathe, the water we drink, the mattresses we sleep on, the carpets we walk on, the radiation from power lines, fertilizers, pesticides, preservatives, hormones in our food, the overuse of anti-inflammatory medications and antibiotics… and much more.

In his book, *Clean*, Dr. Alejandro Junger writes:

… toxins, … enter your body and corrode it from the inside. As toxicity accumulates, your body systems are damaged one by one …

Emotional Toxins

These are toxins of the mind. You may never have thought of it this way but toxicity is not limited to food and chemicals. There is another kind of toxicity that is just as dangerous. I am referring to:

1. Toxic thoughts

2. Toxic beliefs

3. Toxic feelings

To quote Dr. Junger, *Stressful thoughts find a way to the weakest part of your body and begin to disrupt functioning.*

And: *The stress of modern life is as much a toxin as the chemicals in our food, water and air.*

Preventing and Cooling Inflammation

It is important for parents to know how to prevent and reduce inflammation by *building non-inflammatory parent-child relationships*. NeuroParenting does just that. Parenting in this way prevents the build-up of emotional toxins in the child's spirit and cools systemic inflammation. The result will be a calm nervous system. The way parents behave and communicate have a huge impact of the child's level of stress and inflammation. Using *functional parenting* together with the supplemental and nutritional benefits from the FIX IT step, stress and systemic inflammation will be considerably reduced. After the first two weeks, parents tell me with much surprise, 'the atmosphere in our home is totally different.'

Your NeuroParenting Toolbox

Historically, the biological factors contributing to inflammation have been given the most attention. Modern doctors are now realizing there is a connection between chronic emotional stress and systemic inflammation. The negative thoughts and feelings, fears and anxieties of a hurting spirit are very powerful triggers for inflammation. Parents can reduce inflammation by reducing emotional stress in the parent-child relationship. It is the parent's responsibility to know how to engage with their children in ways that:

- Do not inflame their nervous system
- Trigger negative thoughts and feelings
- Trigger fight or flight.

NeuroParenting includes skills such as:

- Having non-inflammatory conversations with your children

- Changing the language you use with the child from pro-inflammatory to non-inflammatory language
- Identifying and changing your own inflammatory behaviors and body language
- Knowing how to stimulate balanced chemistry in your child's spirit-body-brain during your normal daily interaction

The next two chapters contain a select sample of NeuroParenting tools described in great detail. They are easy to use and will make a significant difference to FIRING UP and calming down your child's spirit-body-brain chemistry. You can actually begin to use each tool the moment you read about it. You do not need any resources or equipment. You only need the passion and desire to play a skilled role in healing your child. The FIRE IT UP step of the *Parents, Take Charge* Program is unique because while Mom and Dad are using these skills to heal their kids' chemistry, they are healing themselves at the same time.

I have selected eight FIRE IT UP tools to share with you. These tools are arranged under the following two headings:

1. **Healing Conversations**	2. **Healing Behaviors**
(i) Lose the *"You"* Messages	(i) Being Present
(ii) Create a Family Team	(ii) Healing Touch
(iii) Lose the Label	(iii) Breathing
(iv) The Identity Builder	(iv) The Power of Gratitude

So let's begin!

CHAPTER 11
Your Neuroparenting Toolbox – Healing Conversations

His Name is Bill.

He has wild hair, wears a T-Shirt with holes in it, jeans and no shoes, literally his wardrobe for his entire four years of college. He is brilliant. Kind of esoteric and very creative. He became a Christian while attending college.

Across the street from the campus is a very conservative church with well-dressed parishioners. One day Bill decides to go there. He walks in with no shoes, jeans, his T-shirt, and wild hair. The service has already started and so Bill starts down the aisle looking for a seat.

The church is completely packed and he can't find a seat. By now people are looking a little uncomfortable. Bill gets closer and closer to the pulpit, and when he realizes there are no seats, he just squats down on the carpet. (Although perfectly acceptable behavior at a college fellowship, trust me, this action has never happened in this church before!)

By now the people are really uptight and the tension in the air is thick. About this time, the minister realizes that at the back of the church, a deacon is slowly making his way towards Bill. The deacon is an elegant man in his eighties, with silver-gray hair. A godly man, very elegant, very dignified, very courtly. He walks with a cane, and as he starts walking towards this boy, everyone is saying to themselves that they cannot blame him for what he is about to do. How can you expect a man of his age and of his background to understand some college kid on the floor?

> It takes a long while for the deacon to reach the boy. The church is utterly silent except for the clicking of the man's cane. All eyes are focused on him. You cannot even hear the sound of breathing. The minister does not preach the sermon until the deacon has done what he has to do. And then they see the elderly man drop his cane on the floor. With great difficulty, he lowers himself and sits down next to Bill and begins to worship with him so that Bill would not be alone.
>
> Everyone chokes up with emotion. When the minister gains control, he says: "What I am about to preach to you, you will never remember. What you have just seen, you will never forget. Be careful how you live. You may be the only Bible some people will ever read."
>
> *When your children watch you, what are they seeing?*

FIRE IT UP

It is too easy for parents to heave a sigh of relief as they see improvements happening during the FIX IT phase. They believe that now their child is going to be totally healed. This conclusion would be a mistake. Remember, this method is a 3-step program and leaving any one of the steps out could slow or prevent further improvements and even cause the problems to re-emerge.

The third step, **FIRE IT UP**, teaches parents the skills to maintain and continually reinforce the healing process for their children. I refer to these **FIRE IT UP** parenting skills as *NeuroParenting*.

NeuroParenting is a collection of skills and tools that empower parents to interact with their children in ways that will stimulate the kind of neurochemicals that build a healthy spirit-body-brain. These parenting skills and tools are easily incorporated into any daily schedule and lifestyle in a natural way. Parents do not have to restructure their lives to use NeuroParenting. It just becomes the normal way of doing things. There is a tendency for parents to believe that new skills mean more work for them. That is not the case with NeuroParenting, as you will see in the two chapters that follow. The tools I teach are easy, fun to do and will make your lives and the children's lives easier and calmer.

The goals of the NeuroParenting tools described in this chapter and the next are:
   a. To enhance healthy neurochemistry
   b. To prevent the build-up of stress chemistry
   c. To calm the child's nervous system
   d. To prevent chronic fight or flight
   e. To prevent the build-up of systemic inflammation
   f. To build the child's spirit-body-brain resilience

Did you ever consider the way in which you engage with your child, the words you use, and the kind of conversations you have, *can either inflame or heal* your child? Think about the last time you had a stressful day. Did your stress cause you to make a knee-jerk response that you later regretted? Maybe you snapped at someone you love. Did you say something to your child that you later wished you had not said?

Perhaps you made a poor decision because the stress did not allow you to think clearly? Clearly, as a parent you are not expected to do and say all the right things every time. The fact is, though, that you do live in a high-pressure world, which can mess with your chemistry. Your chemistry can make you more anxious, angry, short-tempered, frustrated or irritable than you would like to be, and your behavior messes with the child's chemistry.

Stressed Moms and Dads may unintentionally:
- Use inflammatory language
- Have inflammatory conversations
- Display inflammatory body language

Below are Four Tools for Healing Conversations:

(i) Lose the "You" Messages
(ii) Create a Family Team
(iii) Lose the Label
(iv) The Identity Builder

(i) Lose the *"You"* Messages

You… conversations are inflammatory. It tells the child that they are the problem – there is something wrong with *them*; *they* are making life difficult; *they* are disappointing you. Below are just a few examples of what "you" messages can sound like. Your particular brand of you messages may sound a little different but I think you'll get the idea once you have read these:

"I have told *you* a thousand times that…"
" Don't *you* understand that if *you* continue …"
"That was a bad choice *you* made to …"
" I don't believe this. Did *you* not hear a single thing I said?"
"What about 'don't do that!' did *you* not understand?"
"No! No! No! *You* never ever do that to your sister!"
"Are *you* listening? Do *you* hear me?!"
"How many times have I told *you* not to …"
"*You're* impossible! *You* drive me crazy."
"Hurry up! *You're* late for a change!"
"Why can't *you* ever …"
"Why do *you* always…"
"*You* know *you're* not supposed to do that!"

You may say to me, 'Well, we do need to set boundaries; we do need to tell the kids when they are misbehaving. How do we do that without using the *'you'* word?" Using the 'you' word makes children become defensive and resistant, which works against healthy boundary setting. More importantly though, eventually the child's brain wires messages like, "I always do the wrong things; I'm a problem; I make bad choices; I can't get it right; I'm stupid." Unfortunately, these messages can become the story they believe about themselves, which eventually becomes a self-fulfilling prophecy.

I would recommend that you replace *you* with *we*. Be aware though that used in the wrong way, the word *we* can also be very disparaging. The next tool will show you how to replace *you* with *we* in a positive way. This tool will also give you the skill to set clear boundaries.

(ii) Create a Family Team – Have *"We"* Conversations

The goals of this NeuroParenting tool are to:

- Replace inflammatory language and inflammatory conversations with non-inflammatory, healing conversations
- Replace inflammatory behaviors with healing behaviors
- Teach collaboration
- Teach the family values
- Set clear and healthy boundaries

Reframe the Family as a Team.

Children of all ages understand the team concept. They see sports teams on TV and are involved in team activities at school. When the kids see the family as a team, it changes the way they interact with you and their siblings. It also changes the language and the conversations in the home.

It should be set up in a fun way as follows:

1. Tell the kids that Mom and Dad have decided that the family should be like a team, where everyone is shooting for the same goal posts.
2. Explain why being a team is such a good idea:
    - Team members always help each other, support each other, care about each other.

- Take responsibility for their behavior; always do their very best.
- Help each other become winners.
- Show respect to each other.
- Are honest with each other.
- Have fun together.
- Make good choices.

When you explain to the kids why you think it is a good idea to be a team, you are actually teaching them wonderful life values. These team values are actually the values you want the family to live by.

PARENTS, TAKE CHARGE!

So Mom and Dad, please select them carefully and intentionally to suit your family. These team values will become the way of defusing conflict; they will be the benchmark for all behaviors and for setting boundaries. I recommend that you write the team values you select in large letters on a project sheet and place the sheet in a prominent position for all to see.

3. Brainstorm a name for the family team, a really fun activity. Take a large sheet of project paper or butcher paper and spend time brainstorming the name for the family team. Let their imaginations run wild until you come up with a team name that excites everyone.

From that moment on, all conversations in the family are about the team.

Conversations sound more like: How are *we* doing today? In this family team we support each other. That's not the way we behave as part of a team. It's been a great week for *our* team! It hasn't been a good team day today but *we* can do better tomorrow. Notice that the word *you* has now been replaced by the word *we*.

In the beginning, one of the kids may resist the team idea and may even become angry about it. Gently and firmly continue the team conversations. Do not get into an intellectual discussion with them about it. When they see you are serious about the team, and their siblings are buying into it, they will slowly warm up.

It is up to you as the parents to be the role models and to devise creative and motivational ways of keeping the team concept alive. I recommend having a team meeting – perhaps every Sunday afternoon - to share how the team had performed that week. The family agrees on a score the team has earned for the week. They agree about what they can do to improve their score the following week. Having a team performance chart highly visible in the kitchen or family room can be very useful. Some parents have created a team logo and placed it on team T-shirts.

This Family Team tool is excellent for *setting clear and healthy boundaries* in a non-inflammatory way, using statements such as:

- We're a winning team. Winning teams don't behave in that way.
- In our team we do it this way…
- Let's think about it. Would a member of a winning team do that?

Each child is learning that he or she is an important member of the family team, the team could not succeed without them and they need to earn this position, as does everyone else in the family. In addition, they are learning important team behavior and life values that will benefit them outside the home and for the rest of their lives.

When used in an inspiring, collaborative, coaching manner, (rather than in a punitive way) the family team approach will be far less likely to cause an inflammatory response in the child. One parent told me, *You know you have successfully inculcated this approach when your child tells you… Mom, that's not the way we behave in this team!*

(iii) Lose the Label

The goals of the NeuroParenting tool are:
- To increase the number of healing conversations about your child
- To avoid giving the child an excuse for not being as powerful as he or she can be

In earlier chapters, you have read how strongly I feel about diagnostic labels that, unfortunately, become a part of the child's identity. These labels also become a large part of conversations between parent and child, the child and his siblings, the child and his friends, teacher and child and parents and teachers.

Remove diagnostic labels from any and all of your conversations.

Everyone is speaking about the child, or with the child, in terms of the label that has been hung around his neck! It is no wonder then that for the child, the label becomes, "This is who I am."

I highly recommend that you drop the label or labels your child has been given. Instruct teachers and family members not to use the label. Your child may certainly be displaying some symptoms, and you will need to discuss these symptoms, **but lose the label.**

Teacher-Parent
- David is really having a hard time paying attention lately. Have you had him tested?
- Yes he has been diagnosed with ADHD. It seems to be worse the last few weeks.

Parent-Child
- The teacher says you don't sit in your chair and are disrupting others.
- I can't help it. I've got ADHD.

Sister-Parent
- Just don't tease him; you know it gets him going.
- Mom, David is making me mad. Has he taken his ADHD medication today?

(iv) The Identity Builder

The goals of this tool are to:

- Replace the inflammatory label conversations with healing conversations
- Build your child's self-concept
- Identify your child's unique identity
- Build your child's self-esteem
- Build the child's emotional resilience

Think about the amount of time you spend on noticing the negatives versus the positives in your child. When our children are grappling with problems, that is all we tend to see. Focusing on the problems causes stress, which stimulates unhealthy chemistry and results in anxiety and fear. Our stress and anxiety is then absorbed by our kids and their chemistry is affected. It is vitally important to increase the number of healing conversations you have with your child that focus on his or her strengths and potential. These conversations will help your child build a positive self-image and self-esteem. It will also help rewire the child's brain with a positive story of who he or she is and what he or she is capable of achieving.

See the Potential, Not the Problems

Is your child funny, creative, kind, caring, helpful, generous or loving? Is he a great cook? Is she smart with numbers; does she draw beautifully, love music, keep her room tidy? Make a list of all the special traits your child has and mention those traits to them and to others often.

Watch for opportunities to tell your child things like, "I really love the way you helped your brother with his homework today. That was very kind of you." Or, "You are so funny. You make me laugh. I like that."

Or, "The teacher told me that you are so good at math. That's a great ability to have."

Every time you say something positive, you are helping them build a positive self-image and identity. And you are stimulating neurochemicals that improve your child's ability to learn, feel good and be happy! With the right chemicals flowing through his system, your child will then be able to begin to actualize his potential and increase his strengths.

There is an added bonus! At the same time, by recognizing their strengths and tuning into their potential, as well as speaking out loud about these, you are changing your chemistry, from stress to joy.

> **What you think about and thank about, you bring about.**

Be aware:
- To rewire the brain and the way your child thinks about himself, positive feelings must be consistently reinforced. *The child needs a ration of 5-1 positive to negative messages and experiences and must feel it for at least 10-20 seconds.* Don't allow the child to minimize what you have said or to change the subject. Make sure they are hearing you, absorbing what you have said and feeling good about it.
- Be sure you really mean it. Don't invent something because the child will know you are not being authentic. It is better not to say anything than to say something that is not true.

Now that we've discussed Healing Conversations, let's go to Chapter 12 to explore the other important aspect of your NeuroParenting Toolbox – Healing Behaviors.

CHAPTER 12
Your Neuroparenting Toolbox – Healing Behaviors

Everyone Is Important

During Mark's first month of college, the professor gave his students a pop quiz. Mark was a conscientious student and had breezed through the questions, until he read the last one: "What is the first name of the woman who cleans the school?"

Surely this was some kind of joke? He had seen the cleaning woman several times. She was tall, dark-haired and in her 50's, but how would he know her name? He handed in his paper, leaving the last question blank.

Just before class ended, one student asked if the last question would count toward the quiz grade.

"Absolutely," said the professor. "In your careers, you will meet many people. All are significant. They each deserve your attention and care, even if all you do is smile and say "hello."

Mark never forgot that lesson. He also learned her name was Dorothy.

Do your children feel that you are present when you are with them?

Your NeuroParenting Behaviors

In the previous chapter you learned about non-inflammatory, healing conversations. These conversations need to be accompanied by non-inflammatory behaviors.

Here are four healing behavior tools:

(i) Being Present

(ii) Healing Touch

(iii) Breathing

(iv) The Power of Gratitude

Your children are watching your behavior very closely and they are unconsciously coming to conclusions about themselves based on how they see you behave. They are deciding, *I am important; I am interesting; I am loved; I am irritating; I am annoying; I am boring* … These conclusions are not logical. They are made in the child's nervous system, and will evoke feelings which will then impact their neurochemistry. If your behavior sends the message, *I am worried about you because I think you have problems*, the child will feel unsafe and ill at ease. This can diminish the happy chemicals. If your behavior sends the message, *I love you for who you are*, the child gets a spurt of endorphins, dopamine and oxytocin. That is exactly what NeuroParenting aims to achieve!

(i) Being Present

We live such busy lives, with so many things calling for our attention. The result is that our minds are often in many places at once, thinking about everything we need to get through that day, worrying about how we will achieve our daily goals, multitasking and planning what we need to do next. When we are in that kind of mind space, we can *be with* our children, but not really *be there* with our children. We are not truly present. And their spirit knows this.

I am sure you have had this experience. You are with someone but you sense his or her mind is elsewhere and it makes you feel angry, lonely, negated or sad. The implicit message is that you are not important enough to receive their full attention. You may, or may not, have also noticed the effect this inattentiveness had on your chemistry. Perhaps you shut down emotionally or your heart was beating faster, and you wanted to say, *"Hello! I am here. Look at me. Listen to me. See me!"* This reaction is how children feel when their parents are not truly present.

A participant in one of my workshops told us the story that while doing homework with her five-year-old son, she was also responding to text messages on her cell phone. Her son took her face in his two little hands, turned her away from her cell phone and said, *I hate it when you do that!* She told us that she had pulled away from him, telling him that she just needed to finish her text message and continued typing. She cried while telling us this. She said: "I am crying because I now realize I lost a perfect opportunity to be present and add to the health of my child's spirit, body and brain!"

Being Present – One of the Most Profound Tools of NeuroParenting
Put everything else aside. Stop multitasking. Make eye contact with your child. Touch your child. Let them feel how important they are to you. Let them know how much you love them. Listen, ask questions, empathize and engage meaningfully, with your head, heart and soul.

I received an email from a mom who had been practicing *being present* for a while with her non-verbal autistic child. She wrote, "Being present has changed the energy between Josh and me, in ways that I would not have thought possible."

Being present is a simple tool with profound neurochemical effects. As simple as it is, however, it takes a great deal of discipline on your part to lay aside whatever you are doing and give your child your full attention when they are interacting with you. The pull to answer the cell phone or respond to the text message or chop the onions can be very strong. Remember not to let your attention wander or you won't bring about the neurochemical enhancement you want for your child!

(ii) Healing Touch

Touch is so vital to humans and most of us don't get nearly enough of it. Babies deprived of touch don't develop normally because certain connections in the brain actually disappear. There are many chemical and health benefits of touch. One of these is that it stimulates the body to produce a hormone called *oxytocin*. This hormone makes us feel good about the person we are with, creating bonding and feelings of trust and love. Oxytocin can also induce feelings of optimism and increased self-esteem. Studies show that it can increase generosity and feelings of empathy. Oxytocin has been observed to reduce cortisol in the body, thereby reducing stress. In addition, it has also been shown to calm gastrointestinal inflammation.

Touch is a powerful NeuroParenting tool but it is most important to understand that there are specific ways to touch the child. There are ways that will stimulate the good chemistry and calm the nervous system, and ways not to touch because it arouses stress chemicals. It is, therefore, important that you know *how to touch your children* that will help their nervous system calm and organize itself, so that they can then process information and respond positively. Some children do not like to be touched and you should not force the issue.

Good Touch Techniques
- Apply a firm stroking touch from the neck down the back, while compressing the front of the chest. Do not stroke from the bottom of the back upwards.
- Apply deep pressure from middle of the back to the outside of the shoulder – do both sides.
- Stroke firmly from the shoulder down the outer arm into the top of the hand (not the palm). Keep the pressure constant as you go from shoulder area to hand.
- Place the child's hand between your thumb and index finger – index finger on top and make a gentle kneading motion.

I recommend that you build the opportunity to touch your children – and spouse - into your daily routine. Do it in an informal manner, whenever the moment presents itself. Perhaps you are sitting next to them on the couch watching TV; they are sitting opposite you and telling you something or just before homework. Casually reach out and touch them for a few minutes, using one of the techniques described above. At first they may think it is strange, but they will soon get used to it and will probably begin asking you for a back rub because it feels so good.

(iii) Breathing

Deep breathing is a remarkable tool for you, as well as your children, to learn and use several times a day. Use it to defuse some tension or a meltdown, as well as informally building it into your day, saying, "Okay, kids, it's time for us to breathe in some wonderful oxygen."

Breathing has many important benefits:
- Helps the body rid itself of toxins
- Calms the mind and body
- Gives the brain more oxygen for better performance
- Helps to focus better -to think more clearly
- Becomes a skill for self control when the child feels agitated
- Flicks the switch from high alert to low in a matter of seconds

The 6-3-6-Breathing Exercise:
Be aware that deep breathing always begins with a full exhalation. This may sound strange but it is important! You can't inhale fully until you empty your lungs completely. Sit up straight. Be sure to relax your shoulders. Breathe in and out through your nose. Breathe in slowly counting to six, hold for the count of three, and then breathe out for the count of six. Belly out when you breathe in, belly in when you breathe out. Repeat several times each time you do this.

Make Deep Breathing a Way of Life!
We tend to forget to breathe deeply. Post sticky-notes with the word "Breathe" around your house, on your desk or in your car. Stoplights make a good place to practice breathing. When you teach children to use deep breathing regularly you are not only improving their health but also empowering them with a life skill. Four year old Max has serious nutritional irregularities, food allergies and intestinal fungus. This was causing unpredictable and fierce outbursts and meltdowns. One day, after one of these meltdowns, he told his mom it was like *'my engine goes on high and I can't stop it.'* We taught him the breathing technique. Some days later he came home from school and told mom,

'my engine started to go on high in class but I breathed and it went away.' This young child not only learned that he has control but he also has a tool that will benefit him in many situations going forward in his life.

(iv) The Healing Power of Gratitude

Much research is now being conducted on the neurochemistry of gratitude. Scientists confirm that practicing gratitude actually alters the neurochemistry of our brain, decreases physical pain, increases alertness, supports better, deeper sleep and promotes overall well-being. Several studies have shown the more grateful a person is, the less depressed they are. Who would have believed that true feelings of gratitude could have such immense benefits?! Since NeuroParenting is about changing brain chemistry for the better, it makes sense that practicing true gratitude would be an important NeuroParenting tool for your tool box.

Be aware that there is an important difference between a fleeting thought of gratitude and deep gratitude felt in your spirit. These feelings of deep gratitude occur when we stand still for a moment and let ourselves feel deeply grateful for something – or everything. Unless you are already practicing deep gratitude as a normal and natural way of life, feeling true gratitude requires that you change the way you look at your life. When you look at what you have and wish that things would be different than what they are, you are switching on chemicals that will create emotional pain and suffering. The more you focus on what makes you unhappy and on what is missing, the more you are interfering with the happy chemicals and the unhappier you will get. The bad news is that this unhappy chemistry eventually becomes wired in your brain so that you automatically think that way. The good news is that practicing gratitude can help you stimulate the happy chemicals and rewire your brain to quickly and easily tune into the blessings of your life.

Be aware: It is not possible for parents to teach the practice of gratitude to their children, unless they themselves practice it.

Teaching and Practicing Gratitude
a. My Children's Gratitude Journal

Teach your children about the concept of gratitude and what it means. I like the narrative that sounds something like this: *Each day is filled with some things that make you happy and some things that may make you frustrated or not so happy. Sometimes we forget to notice the good things. Gratitude is about always noticing the good things and feeling happy and grateful that these good things happened.*

Each evening before switching their lights off, sit at each child's bedside and ask him or her to tell you three things they are grateful for that happened that day. At first they may find this difficult but they will soon get the hang of it. Make it a rule never to let your kids go to sleep at night without doing this gratitude exercise. They will go to sleep on good chemistry and wake up feeling positive. It is also an amazing tool for them to use all through their lives. After this nightly exercise, record the things they were grateful for in a gratitude journal – *My Children's Gratitude Journal.* This journal tells a very special story.

b. My Personal Gratitude Journal

Keep a personal Gratitude Journal on your bedside table. Just before going to sleep, write about what you are grateful for from that day. It is even better if you and your husband can share your personal gratitudes of the day with each other. You will be surprised what a positive impact this practice can have on your relationship and your attitude towards each other and life in general.

Your children are watching your every move.

Think about this question:
What are my children learning from my behavior?

The NeuroParenting Toolbox is only as effective as your commitment to use it. The tools in the last two chapters are easy to incorporate into your normal way of life. Try them and then let me know about how this changes your life!

Finally, there is one last missing piece of the healing puzzle. Chapters 13 and 14 will tell you what this is.

CHAPTER 13
Mom, Dad, It Starts With You

It's In The Eyes.

It was a bitter, cold evening in northern Virginia many years ago. The old man's beard was glazed by winter's frost while he waited for a ride across the river. The wait seemed endless. His body became numb and stiff from the frigid north wind. He heard the faint, steady rhythm of approaching hooves galloping along the frozen path.

Anxiously, he watched as several horsemen rounded the bend. He let the first one pass by without trying to get his attention. He ignored all the horsemen until finally the last rider neared the spot where the old man sat like a snow statue.

As this rider drew near, the old man caught the rider's eye and when he stopped, he said, "Sir, would you mind giving an old man a ride to the other side? There isn't a passageway by foot."

Reining in his horse, the rider replied, "Sure. Climb aboard."

The horseman took the old man not just across the river, but to his destination, which was just a few miles away. As they neared the tiny but cozy cottage, the horseman's curiosity caused him to ask, "Sir, why on such a bitter night did you wait for the last rider? What if I had refused and left you there?"

> The old man lowered himself slowly down from the horse, looked the rider straight in the eyes, and replied, "I reckon I know people pretty good. I looked into the eyes of the other riders and immediately saw they did not care about me. It would have been useless even to ask them for a ride. But when I looked into your eyes, kindness and compassion were evident. I knew immediately that your gentle spirit would welcome the opportunity to help me in my time of need."
>
> Those heartwarming comments touched the horseman deeply. "I'm most grateful for what you have said," he told the old man. "May I never get too busy in my own affairs that I fail to respond to the needs of others with kindness and compassion."
>
> With that, Thomas Jefferson turned his horse around and made his way back to the White House.
>
> *What do your children see in your eyes? Fear and worry or pride and joy?*

This may be the most important chapter of the whole book!

I am in awe of how dedicated parents are as they travel on this challenging journey, looking for a way to remove the problems their children wrestle with. I want you, Moms and Dads, to know that you inspire me! I respect your dedication to freeing that amazing child behind the problems. I want you also to know that I understand the stress of parents. Every day I see moms and dads with hurting spirits. I see their pain and listen to their hopes and dreams. I know how hard it is to have a happy and light spirit when your child is struggling to feel good, to learn, and to enjoy life.

When you read the contents of this chapter, be aware that under no circumstances am I blaming or criticizing you, but rather wanting to inform and empower you so that you can make your dreams for your children come true.

Here is something for all parents to think about:

If you have high levels of stress, this condition may be making it more difficult for your children to overcome their challenges.

Not only does your stress affect your own chemistry - it also impacts the chemistry of your children. And not in a good way!

We Can Sense Each Other's Feelings, Fears, and Vulnerabilities

The parents who attend my workshops complete a registration form on which I ask, "Why are you attending this workshop?" They write about being frustrated because they do not know how to alleviate the burdens that make life so difficult for their beloved children and the family. The words they use to describe themselves are: *confused, angry, afraid and overwhelmed*. The word *desperate* appears on almost every other registration form.

It is a scientifically proven fact that your children absorb your stress.

These feelings are totally understandable. The problem is that when you are stressed, your kids know it. They know when you feel desperate. They know it because of your body language, your gestures, the expression on your face, the tone of your voice, the tense way you interact with them. All of these scream the message that Mommy is stressed, or Daddy is stressed! They don't know this fact intellectually. *It is not a cognitive knowing – it is a neural knowing. Their nervous system knows it.* Dr. Stephen Porges is recognized for the remarkable research he has done on this kind of knowing which he refers to as *neuroception*. He defines this as: detection without awareness. In other words, kids just know.

It is actually your child's nervous system that is interpreting your gestures, tone of voice, and facial expressions as being safe or unsafe. If what they see makes them feel safe, the nervous system will be calm. If your behavior and conversation causes them to feel vulnerable or unsafe, their nervous system will become aroused. They will then either mobilize or shut down, in other words, go into fight or flight. What you will see is that they have an angry outburst (fight) or withdraw (flight); play victim (flight) or persecutor (fight). *Now you have an interaction between you and your child that is igniting unhealthy stress chemistry, and the ensuing inflammation, for you both.*

Bottom line: You cannot hide your stress. As the story at the beginning of the chapter tells us, "It's in your eyes." You cannot role-play or pretend you are not stressed. They know it deep inside. They see through your pretense. The important thing to remember is that seeing you stressed will cause your kids to feel stressed. I see this reaction between parents and children every day and it is difficult to watch because I know it will keep everyone stuck in a dysfunctional state of arousal.

Kids can't engage positively with others– or learn– when they are in a state of arousal. It is also difficult to calm a child having a temper tantrum or a meltdown when their arousal system has kicked into overdrive. There is no point in expecting them to learn or attend or focus when this happens because they simply can't. There is no point in punishing them or yelling at them or explaining logically why their behavior is unacceptable because, once they are aroused, they cannot "hear" you or think logically. It is only when the child's nervous system begins to calm that he can process information and self-correct.

Interacting with your child in a stress-less way will help him maintain a calm nervous system.

It is vitally important for parents and teachers to understand how to engage with kids in ways that will prevent, manage and reduce stress, promote calm and prevent nervous system arousal

Here's the challenge – it starts with you!

One of the most vital aspects of this journey to making your child well is that you are well. It is not possible for you, Mom or Dad, (or the teacher) to promote a calm spirit-body-brain in your child if you are stressed and aroused. Why?

Your chemistry affects their chemistry.

Because the way a parent with a happy, calm spirit communicates and behaves is vastly different to the way a stressed parent, or teacher, sounds, looks and behaves. Your children need to experience you as parenting them with the behaviors that come from your happy, healthy spirit-body-brain.

Your happy serotonin stimulates their happy serotonin. When your dopamine, oxytocin, endorphins, epinephrine, norepinephrine and other important hormones and neurotransmitters are in balance, that will help to stimulate and balance theirs. The result will be an environment of calm, serenity, love, bonding and emotional safety. You do not want your high cortisol levels to increase their cortisol levels and result in fight or flight responses from you both.

Out of the Mouths of Babes.

As part of my research to discover the effects of stress on children, I conducted a focus group with kids between seven and eleven years of age. (None of the participants attended special needs schools. They also all came from middle to upper-class environments). I wanted to understand what stress meant to them. Some of the questions I asked them were: "How do you know you are stressed? What happens when you feel stressed? What do you do to try and cope with your stress?" I was impressed by the insightfulness of their responses. It struck me, though, how sad it was that seven to eleven-year-old children were already aware of feeling stressed!

These kids were very vocal about the fact that they are super-aware when their parents feel stressed. According to them, this stress makes them feel, "afraid and helpless." One seven-year old told me, "When my mommy is stressed, I feel sick." Another said, "I want to take her stress away and help her but I don't know how, so I get stressed too." Yet another child said, "I am afraid because I don't know what my dad will do next – will he shout at me or just be quiet and not speak?" An eleven-year-old boy said, "As long as my parents or my teacher don't take their stress out on me, I can handle it. But they usually do take it out on me and then I feel bad."

In answer to my questions, *What happens to you when you feel stressed?* And, *How do you know you are stressed?* one child said, (while using his hand to indicate a movement from his belly up to his chest), "When I am stressed it's like a volcano … it starts at the bottom of my tummy and it grows and grows … and then someone just says hello to me and I burst out crying."

This is how others described what happens to them when they feel stressed:

"I feel cold and get like a tight feeling in my head."

"I feel like puking."

"I feel helpless and afraid."

"I fight with my brother."

"I don't know what to do so I go to my bedroom and hit myself with my pillow."

The responses went on and on. These youngsters did not have to hesitate for a second; they did not have to think about what stress is like for them – they could answer this question immediately! After each question I posed, all the little hands flew up, each wanting a chance to share how stress feels for them. What I found so interesting is how they spoke about their stress with such candor. They did not care that the TV cameras and crew were there filming the focus group for a medical program; they did not care that there were many strangers in the audience watching them and listening to them. It was as if they were glad to have the opportunity to speak openly about their stress to someone who wanted to listen.

Listen Up! Here's what the children are telling us!

They know when their mommies and daddies and teachers are stressed; they feel it and they absorb it. They asked me why the adults around them don't deal with their own stress and, "Why does it just go on and on." Children don't understand why their parents are not happy, relaxed, calm, centered and filled with laughter and joy; all they know is that their parents' stress makes them feel anxious and insecure. It robs them of their ability to feel the joy of being a carefree child.

There is a direct relationship between stress and joy. The higher your stress levels are, the lower the amount of joy you are able to feel for yourself or give to others. The amount of joy your children experience when they are with you is linked to the amount of stress you exude – the higher your stress, the lower their joy. It is up to all of us to *Take*

Charge of our stress so that we do not steal the joy of our children (and students) or make them feel unsafe.

> *As a parent or teacher, take a few moments to ask yourself:*
> *What are my kids absorbing from me – stress or joy?*

NeuroParenting

In the previous chapters you learned eight FIRE IT UP NeuroParenting tools. The FIRE IT UP tools are unique because they are designed to give parents the ability to play a major role in healing their children *as part of their normal routine*. Instead of (or in addition to) taking your children to all kinds of therapies, you can incorporate NeuroParenting into your daily interaction with your kids. You become the child's coach. The tools you learned in the previous chapters have a dual effect - they are stimulating healing chemistry, not only for your children but also for you. The FIRE IT UP tools are great to use with all kids, irrespective of whether they are dealing with symptoms or not.

Here's the Challenge

There's a critically important issue that must be addressed before you can use the wonderful healing FIRE IT UP tools effectively with your children.

> *Helping your children overcome their challenges starts with you*
> *recognizing and addressing your own stress level.*

If you suspect that you are chronically stressed, you are faced with having to make a crucial choice. You can say, "I can't help it," or you can learn how to reverse out of stress, press the reset button, get off the stress treadmill, change gears and respond to life in a stress-less way. And then watch the wonderful changes in your children!

Your children cannot choose a stress-less way of life … if you don't!

Do you remember the story at the start of Chapter Nine? The Master told his disciples, *It is nothing more than a problem. Do not run away from it. Deal with it. Take the bull by the horns.*

If you believe your stress levels are too high, if you believe your kids "see it in your eyes," the next chapter will show you exactly how to take the bull by the horns and reboot *YOUR* spirit-body-brain.

CHAPTER 14
Parent, Heal Thyself

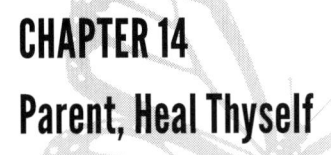

> **Do You Know About The Pacific Salmon?**
>
> As these fish thrash about and struggle upstream to spawn, there is a surge of cortisol in their bodies. The increased levels of this potent stress hormone, provides the fish with the energy they need to fight the current. But the high level of this hormone also leads the salmon to stop eating. Their digestive tracts wither away. Their immune systems break down. And after laying their eggs, they die of exhaustion and infection, their bodies worn out by the journey.
>
> Salmon cannot help being stressed out. They are programmed to die. Their systems are propelled into overdrive by evolutionary design.
>
> *Aren't we blessed that we have the power to choose the way we want to live our lives!*

The Pacific Salmon have no choice. We do.

As humans, even though we have a choice not to let stress destroy us, many of us continue to pile on the stress and then suffer the consequences when the body's biological mechanisms cannot cope. As a result, there's an enormous increase in all kinds of stress-related illness in adults. Millions of adults have reached such high stress levels their body is saying, "Enough! I can't do this anymore."

Falling into this kind of self-made trap is a personal choice. We are, after all, thinking, informed adults who have the right to do what we please with our lives. However, when our choice to be stressed and push ourselves to dangerous limits begins to affect our children, there's a problem.

Parent, Heal Thyself

FIND IT	FIX IT	FIRE IT UP

The one question I am asked the most every day is, "How can I help my child?" And my answer is, *It begins with you helping yourself first.* On a plane, you are instructed that, in the event of a crash, you must put on your own oxygen mask before helping your children. When you are not well because you are stressed, when you are stressed because you are not well, when you are taking all kinds of medication, your ability to be fresh, happy, exciting, energetic, passionate, and funny and relaxed around your children, is reduced. If you want to help your children learn easily and feel good, begin by checking your own stress levels, and if they are high, FIX IT.

The Spirit-Body-Brain Stress Continuum

There is a spirit-body-brain health and stress continuum that goes from balanced and healthy to unbalanced and hurting. I will describe these so that you can assess where *you* are on the continuum.

1. If you are on the far left, you are feeling wonderful. You are happy, healthy and alert. Your spirit-body-brain are dancing together in perfect harmony. If that description is true for you, I salute you!

2. Moving along to the right on the continuum – your spirit is stressed. You struggle to feel blessed, positive and cheerful.

   Instead, you may feel (check those that apply to you):

   - Moody, cranky, irritable
   - Down, "out of sorts," unmotivated
   - Lethargic
   - Low stress tolerance
   - Anxious
   - Forgetful
   - Unfocused

3. Further to the right, your stress level has now begun to affect the body and brain. Now you have some physical symptoms such as:

   - Muscular aches and pains
   - Bloating
   - Insomnia
   - Weight problems

- Headaches
- Brain fog
- Digestive problems
- Allergies
- Sleep problems
- Teeth grinding

4. On the far right end of the continuum, the continual spirit-body-brain stress has caused more serious physical conditions:

    - Thyroid issues
    - Blood sugar imbalance
    - Decreased bone density
    - Decrease in muscle tissue
    - Increased blood pressure
    - Compromised immune system
    - Inflammatory responses in the body
    - Increased fat to stomach area, which is associated with greater health problems than if fat is deposited in other areas of the body - heart disease, higher levels of bad cholesterol (LDL), and lower levels of good cholesterol (HDL), among others.
    - Cognitive / memory problems

If you find yourself somewhere between points two and four on this continuum, your stress levels are out of whack and have thrown important hormones and neurotransmitters off balance. It is time for YOU to FIX YOU.

You Can Choose a Happy or Unhappy Spirit

I cannot know about all the possible things that may be hurting your spirit, *but I do know of one* – your child is hurting. You long for your child to be able to feel good. And while he hurts, so do you. I know this fact from personal experience as a parent and grandparent.

Your child needs you to have a happy, healthy spirit.

Your brain chemistry plays a vital role in whether you have a happy or an unhappy spirit. You can *Take Charge* of these chemicals. You do not have to let the chemistry take charge of you. You can actually influence your own neurochemistry and stimulate either happy or unhappy chemicals and produce a happy or unhappy spirit. Neuro-transmitters are the brain's messengers. Their job is to carry messages between the brain cells, allowing them to communicate with one another. Acetylcholine, dopamine, serotonin, epinephrine, norepinephrine and endorphins, for example, play a role in carrying happy messages. The problem is that stress chemistry interferes with these happy messengers. It throws them off-balance, causes them to fall behind on their happy deliveries and deliver sad messages instead.

Your task is to reset this balance, which can actually be fun to do!

Reset your Chemistry

    a. Fix Your Body and Your Brain Will Follow

    b. Stop the Cortisol Build-Up

    c. Create a Personal Dream Board

a. Fix Your Body and Your Brain Will Follow.
My recommendation is for you to start by fixing your gut. Find a skilled functional nutritionist and fix your digestive and nutritional

issues first. You will probably find that many, or perhaps even all of your symptoms, will improve or disappear when you take this step. Here's why.

Your gut is your second brain. The brain in your head and your gut are interconnected, so when the one hurts so does the other. Until now, we have always believed that the brain determines whether you are happy or sad. We have now discovered that the gut is more responsible than we ever imagined for mental well-being and how we feel. A hundred million neurotransmitters line the length of the gut. These are exactly the same major neurotransmitters that are found in the brain— including serotonin, dopamine, glutamate, norepinephrine and nitric oxide, as well as enkephalins, described as the body's natural opiates.

Working with a good functional nutritionist can be an enlightening and life-enhancing experience. You will learn how what you are eating is harming you or healing you. You will be given the correct rebalancing supplements. You will be educated about what the tests show and about which supplements you need to take to reset your chemistry. You will learn to eat in a way that will enhance and balance your chemistry. You will begin to understand exactly how what goes in your mouth converts into emotions and behavior. You will understand why certain vitamin and minerals deficiencies make it harder for you to manage stress. Most importantly, you will learn about inflammatory and anti-inflammatory foods – which inflammatory foods to take off your supermarket list and out of your pantry!

> **Poor digestive health can trigger a whole cascade of negative effects in your spirit-body-brain.**

b. Stop the Cortisol Build-Up

If you know that you are chronically stressed and if you want to help your child, yourself and your family, your goal is to lower your cortisol levels. The key is to do the opposite of whatever creates cortisol. When you do that, these healthier actions will rewire your brain for more serotonin guided feelings and behaviors.

You will soon find that instead of being cortisol cranky, you are serotonin serene. This is the best gift you can give yourself, your children and your family.

How to Stop Your Cortisol Build-Up

Here are some activities that are really easy and enjoyable to do. These activities will stop the cortisol build-up and spark serotonin and other healthy chemistry.

i. Move, Move, Move. Build movement into your life. Buy yourself a pedometer. Find a friend who wants to do the same and each evening check your pedometers and compare the number of steps you have each taken that day. Find more ways to increase your daily movements. Make the bed, walk the dog, do stairs, not elevators, park a fair distance from where you are going and power walk to your destination. Find an activity that you like, take up a sport. Movement is vital to support your biochemistry, regulate your brain chemicals and stimulate the happy neurotransmitters.

ii. Breathe, Breathe, and Breathe. Set your alarm on your cell phone or find an app that reminds you to do some deep breathing. Taking twelve deep breaths several times a day is extremely healing for the body – it can release endorphins in your body, which will increase your sense of well-being and make you feel more at ease.

iii. Visit or call friends. Positive interactions with others are a great way to reset your chemistry. Spend time with upbeat people who laugh a lot. Steer away from cynics and people who inflame you and are toxic to your well-being.

iv. Manage time, create doable daily targets. Avoid unrealistic overloads.

v. Find time for stress-relievers: relax, get a massage, listen to music, take a walk, buy a boxing bag, give things away, help others in need, practice meditation or yoga.

vi. Consciously decide each morning what you can do to build fun and laughter into your day. Laughter is a miracle drug.

vii. Pet your pooch. There is much research showing the chemical benefits of spending time with your pets.

viii. Make sleep a priority. Go to bed on time. Have a slow-down period each evening before bed. Sleep is a powerful and natural way to recharge and repair your brain and your cells.

ix. Practice gratitude. Find 30 things to be grateful for each day. Write them in a gratitude journal before you go to sleep.

x. Keep a journal. Journaling is an extremely effective tool to help you focus and relax.

xi. Visualize your Dream Board many times in the day. This will remind you that you are on an inspiring and meaningful journey. (see step 3 below)

c. Create a Personal Dream Board

Did you know that the ability to use our imaginations and create dreams for ourselves is what separates us from animals? Unlike animals, we have the mental ability to visualize something and to create mental pictures. We can even see movies in our mind's eye. What an incredible ability our visualizing talents are! They can, however, become a two-edged sword because these images change our chemistry for better or worse. We need to be careful what mental pictures we create. Negative images trigger unhealthy biochemistry and build stress. Parents tell me they are troubled by negative, scary thoughts and images, about their children's problems and what their children's future will be. As a worried parent, it is easy to slip into the habit of picturing the worst. This negative imagery is very destructive to your spirit. *Creating a dream board is an extremely powerful tool to change the thoughts and images you have in your mind and reset your chemistry.*

The Power of a Dream Board

A personal dream is a mental picture that changes your chemistry. It gives your life purpose and meaning and lets your spirit soar. I hope you are able to answer *Yes!* to all these questions.

1. Do you have a dream of how you would ideally like to see yourself in two years? In five years? In ten years? *Can you actually see a picture of this in your brain?* Does this dream put a fire in your belly? Is it like a huge magnifying force that pulls you into the future?

2. Is this dream like a beacon for you so that every single thing you do is done with that dream in mind?

3. Do you use this dream as a tool to keep you going when times are tough?

4. Do you use every opportunity you can find to speak about your dream to your loved ones, friends and colleagues?

5. Have you noticed that when you sit quietly and think about your personal dream, you feel less stressed and you find the courage and energy to do great things?

Over my years in practice, I have seen how the moms and dads who have a personal dream have a sparkle in their eyes, a spring in their step, and passion in their voice. These parents know that being a great parent is not about being a martyr. They "get it" that being a great parent is also about being your own person. It is about living your own inspired, purposeful and meaningful life. Having a personal purpose creates the kind of healthy biochemistry you will need if you are going to be a powerful force in healing your child.

How a Personal Dream Changes Your Chemistry

Nothing happens unless first a dream.
– Carl Sandburg

We are what we are and where we are because we have first imagined it.
– Donald Curtis

Where there is no vision, the people perish.
– Proverbs 29:18

The more often you let yourself visualize that wonderful dream in your mind and the more you speak about it, the more excited you become about achieving this dream. Excitement and passion are feelings created by the happy chemicals, which also give you the courage and inspiration you need. Imagine that! By visualizing an exciting personal dream, you are able to give yourself a natural chemical high!

In the Appendix, I have outlined the step-by-step process for creating a dream board. Parents have shared the most amazing stories with me of how their dream board changed their lives. I highly recommend you create one for yourself.

Remember that your children absorb your stress. You owe it to them and yourself to FIND IT, FIX IT and FIRE yourself UP so that the future holds great health and joy for you all.

CHAPTER 15
Pulling It All Together

Your Take Charge! Check List

1. You've checked your child's spirit-body-brain health status.
2. You are in the process of treating any irregularities that were revealed.
3. You've checked your own spirit-body-brain health status.
4. You are in the process of treating your own health issues.
5. You and your children are taking the five basic supplements the body needs.
6. You have identified and removed inflammatory foods from the family's diet.
7. You are using non-inflammatory language and having healing conversations with your kids.
8. You are aware of your behaviors and are displaying non-inflammatory, healing behavior.

9. You have created a Home Team approach and given the team a name.
10. You have dropped "the label(s)."
11. You are using The Identity Builder as a way of building the child's esteem, identity and spirit.
12. You are fully present in every interaction with your children.
13. You are using touch and breathing with your children.
14. You never go to sleep or let the kids go to sleep without doing the gratitude activity.
15. You have created your Personal Dream Board.
16. You incorporate stress relievers into your normal daily routine.
17. Something inside of you has started to shift – from anxiety and overwhelm, to calm and serene.
18. You are seeing positive changes in yourself and your children.

CHAPTER 16
Are Your Values Helping or Hindering?

One evening an old Cherokee told his grandson about a battle that goes on inside people.

He said, "My son, the battle is between two wolves inside us all...

"One is Evil. It is anger, envy, jealousy, sorrow, regret, greed, arrogance, self-pity, guilt, resentment, inferiority, lies, false pride, superiority, and ego.

"The other is good. It is joy, peace, love, hope, serenity, humility, kindness, benevolence, empathy, generosity, truth, compassion and faith."

The grandson thought about it for a minute and then asked his grandfather, "Which wolf wins?"

The old Cherokee simply replied, "The one you feed."

Which wolf are YOU feeding?

Who's in Your Driver's Seat?

In Chapter I, I wrote *"Behind the layers of learning, behavior and mood issues that so many children grapple with, there is a problem-free child with a healthy body, brain and spirit."* Parents, *Take Charge* is about how to liberate the resilient, self-confident, lively, spirited child within

– a child who can learn easily, behave appropriately and feel good. *Parents, Take Charge* is about healing from the inside-out as opposed to from the outside-in. It is also about the powerful role that stress and pressure play in throwing a child's spirit-body-brain off balance. Stress sets the stage for the current epidemic of learning, behavior and mood challenges that so many children grapple with.

I would like to close by taking the issue of stress and pressure one step further by speaking about a condition that society, organizations, schools, businesses, churches, families and individuals suffer from, which is "the tyranny of the ego."

Just as we have good or toxic stress and good or toxic inflammation, so we have good or toxic ego. The behaviors, the beliefs and the values of too much ego cause stress, which then presses the trigger on disease. When our ego takes control of our lives, we become defensive, arrogant, judgmental and self-righteous. When our ego is in the driver's seat, we live by superficial values that cause us to experience high levels of stress, which upsets the balance of our biochemistry. When we respond to the world with too much ego, we release unhealthy chemicals into the body and the brain.

The flip side of ego is spirit. When our healthy, happy spirit is in the driver's seat, we are in harmony with others and with life. We respond to every situation with openness and humility and we are in touch with a larger purpose for our lives. When we interact with others from our spirit, we are happy, inspired, curious, authentic, honest, respectful, collaborative, compassionate, and true to ourselves, which is where our health lies.

> **The key to our health and well-being lies in our spirit.**

The behaviors of a healthy spirit stimulates the release of essential chemicals, which give us health and well-ness. Ego does not feel the kind of passion, happiness and joy that spirit feels. Too much ego makes us sick – and causes us to try and find happiness in superficial and toxic ways.

Healthy Versus Toxic Values

Millions of children are experiencing unacceptably high levels of poor health, psychological disorders, anxiety, fear, anger, depression, substance abuse, suicide, learning, behavior and mood problems.

One of the most critical causative factors of all these problems is that we teach our children that their self-worth is based on their academic, social and athletic achievement, not on who they are as human beings.

This kind of thinking places great pressure on them.

If you are a sensitive kid growing up in today's high-pressure world, you might want to say something like, "Hey, I feel overwhelmed and anxious; there's too much pressure. Just back off. I can't be all you want me to be, in the way you want me to be! I can't be perfect. I can't be great at everything. You're making me feel bad. *I just need you to be okay with who I am.*"

Even kids who do cope with high stress and pressure can often find, after many years, that coping with such stress eventually catches up with them. Think about teenagers and adults who develop stress-related emotional and physical conditions, need medications to control their symptoms and who become alcoholics or turn to drugs. These kids have lost contact with their healthy spirit. They become stressed parents and create a lifestyle that wires their children for stress.

Kids live in a high pressure world that has been created, and is constantly reinforced, by educators, media and parents. From the moment of birth onwards, parents and educators place enormous pressure on children, academically, socially, emotionally and on the sports field. They are expected to excel at everything they do. Children often feel a responsibility to live up to these expectations. If they don't, they believe they are a disappointment and a failure.

If you listen to the conversations of parents at social gatherings, it is almost always about how well the child is doing in school or on the sports field. They speak about how bright and creative and successful the child is, about the trophies they have won, the grades they achieve, their outstanding test scores and their acceptance into prestigious schools. I have yet to hear a parent talk about how compassionate his child is or the community service the child does or what a grounded, responsible person the child is. Being a great kid is measured by achievement and performance. The child's worth is measured by *doing*, not by *being*. They never receive trophies for being kind and caring, for helping others less fortunate than themselves, for seeing the world through their own eyes, for showing respect, for their collaborative abilities, for challenging a useless status quo, for innovative solutions or for their dreams of greatness. They rarely get recognition just for trying or doing the very best they are capable of doing. And if they do, this recognition is seen as a pity trophy. In response to the question, "How is your son doing," I have never personally heard a parent say, "Thank you for asking. He is such a joy to us. We just love the way he sees the world so differently and we are learning so much from him each day."

The Pressure-cooker Values of Today's Society

I am deeply concerned about some values held by society in general and supported by many parents and educators. These values are currently creating toxic levels of pressure for all children. It is true that there are many stressful situations or events in life that parents simply cannot influence or change. But there are also many things parents can do to ensure that their children are not dealing with unnecessary pressure. Parents can't change the values of society but they most definitely can be responsible for their own family values and for choosing schools that have healthy, non toxic values. Let's examine some of these values:

1. The Achievement Value. Is Yours Healthy or Toxic?

Toxic Value: High achievement is all that matters.

Healthy Value: Doing your very best is all that matters.

Think about it. The pressure and high expectations start in infancy and then ramp up. It starts with parents checking to see if their infant has reached his different developmental milestones sooner than other infants. Children as young as three or four years of age are being tutored in order to be admitted to the very best kindergarten programs. Kids are being asked to leave preschools because their behaviors do not match the school's definition of what is appropriate. There is no more time in schools for exercise, being outdoors and just having silly fun – only for academic learning and achievement.

We all want our kids to achieve in as many spheres of life as possible. I agree that we must encourage them to strive for achievement – based on their unique capabilities. However, when parents and educators live by values that are more concerned about grades and performance than about health and well-being, they are creating toxic pressure. Sure, everyone pays lip service to the importance of the child's well-being.

The reality is that far more emphasis is placed on rewarding kids for greater achievement than for empathy and kindness, self-belief and compassion and resilience and courage.

Achievement Stress

Several researchers have identified warning signs of achievement-stress in kids. As you read this list, notice how the traditional healthcare practitioner would most likely diagnose and treat these symptoms as being ADHD, mood disorder, defiance, low motivation, or all of the above. Yet these symptoms are actually signs of achievement stress. If you deal with the achievement-stress, the symptoms will go away! For example, you could ensure the child goes to a school with a relaxed classroom environment, a school that encourages the child to be the best they can be and that provides work that is within the child's "comfort zone" in terms of success. If you medicate these children for ADHD or a mood disorder without dealing with the achievement stress, the untreated achievement stress will continue to cause spirit-body-brain pain. So why do we not deal with achievement stress? Because we have a toxic value that high achievement is all that counts in life.

Some achievement-stress warning signs:
1. Overactive or distracting behaviors (fidgeting, making unnecessary trips to the bathroom, nervous tics, jumping from task to task, showing difficulty in concentrating, being prone to accidents, sighing)
2. Major change in attitude or temperament (irritability, lack of enthusiasm, carelessness)
3. Withdrawal or angry outbursts
4. Complaints of fatigue and vague illnesses
5. Problems sleeping

6. Headaches or stomach aches
7. Increase in allergic or asthmatic attacks
8. Avoidance of school or testing situation by direct refusal or convenient illness (an unnecessary trip to the nurse)
9. Loss of appetite or excessive eating
10. Nail biting
11. Antisocial or disruptive behaviors
12. Sudden dramatic increase or decrease in effort in school
13. Drug use or abuse

2. The Competition Value – is Yours Healthy or Toxic?

Toxic value: Strive to be better than others - socially, athletically, and academically

Healthy Value: Strive to be the very best YOU

We live in a competitive world. Kids are competing every moment of every day and in every way, no matter how young or old they are. The differences between healthy and toxic competition are the values that drive it. There are different forms of competition. Check your values in each of these below:

(i) Kids compete for each other's attention.

Every child wants to be popular; they want others to want them as a friend, and they want to be friends with the most popular kids in school. Being rejected by others is a child's worst nightmare. There is even a new diagnostic label – *Facebook Depression* - apparently caused by feeling inadequate due to having fewer Facebook friends than others!

The emphasis on being popular is made even worse if they know popularity is important to Mom and Dad. Have you taught your kids that being popular means they are special? Or have you taught them to feel personal pride and to value themselves for who they are?

Check your values – healthy or toxic?

Toxic Value: Move with the inner circle. Be one of the popular kids. Be "cool."

Healthy Value: You are cool just being you.

(ii) **Kids compete athletically.**

Children who have a natural athletic ability are glorified in most schools. They are looked up to, admired and even hero-worshipped by other kids and adults around them. Non-athletic kids wish they could be just like them. Knowing they can't hurts because everyone places such value on athleticism.

Parents, check your values – healthy or toxic?

Toxic Value: Being athletic makes you special.

Healthy Value: Be proud of the strengths you have.

(iii) **Kids compete materialistically.**

Kids are aware of what brand of sneakers and clothes they are wearing, what cell phones they are carrying, what laptop they are using, what cars their parents drive, what electronic gadgets they have … The problem arises when they equate wearing the latest, most high profile brands with being trendy, "cool," and more special than other kids who do not have the materialistic trappings.

Parents, check your values – healthy or toxic?

Toxic Value: I will buy this stuff for my kids so they can be special.

Healthy Value: My kids don't need this stuff to be special. They are special because they are who they are.

I am in favor of buying the newest, popular brand stuff, if you need it, if you can afford it and if you are motivated by an appreciation for top quality. I am not in favor of parents buying this stuff for their kids believing it will help their children get the attention of others or hoping it will help them be a member of the in-crowd. When moms and dads buy the popular things, they do not teach the child to value *whom they are*.

Do you remember the focus group with children that I wrote about in Chapter 13? I asked the children for the three top causes of stress in their lives. Not having the best clothes, sneakers, phones, computers… were amongst the top three worst stressors for these kids. A ten year old girl told us that, *others treat me like a lowly because I don't have an iPhone*. When asked what a 'lowly' was, she said, *like someone that is not as good as others*.

The examples described above are some of the values of society, media and parents that have the potential to create constant high-powered stress and pressure for kids. These toxic values can contribute to the ever-increasing numbers of children with ADD, ADHD, OCD, ODD, depression, bullying, meltdowns, underachievement and low motivation.

It is also the kind of stress and pressure that parents CAN prevent.

Who's in YOUR Driver's Seat?

Do you want your children to be resilient, happy, high achievers who can steer through everyday obstacles and bounce back from setbacks? I am sure the answer is a resounding, *Yes!* Here's the critical question: Is this desire coming from your ego or your strong spirit? If your ego is in the driver's seat, you will see your children as an extension of yourselves. You will want them to achieve because you enjoy the prestige this gives you as the parent. It reflects well on you as their Mom and Dad.

If your spirit is in the driver's seat, then all you want for your child is to become everything he or she is capable of being. Whatever that is, is great. Imagine how empowering and freeing such a value can be for you and your children. I am not saying that we must create a stress-free lifestyle for our kids or protect them from ever feeling pressured. I am asking parents to know the difference between healthy or toxic values that ignite healthy or toxic stress. I am asking parents to stop for a moment and think about:

- Who's in my driver's seat most of the time? My ego or my spirit?
- Are the values I teach my children ego-driven or spirit-driven values?
- Will my values ignite my child's spirit or will these values inflame and stress him?
- Am I living by materialistic, educational, social, societal and athletic values that are causing unnecessary stress and pressure for my children?
- Do I need to re-examine my values?

Are Your Values Helping or Hindering?

- Do I need to make a personal values adjustment to reduce my own and my child's stress?

  I ask moms and dads to consider avoiding or adjusting these values of the ego:

- High achievement is the only thing that counts.
- You must be better than others - socially, athletically and academically.
- Move with the inner circle. Be one of the popular kids. Be "cool."
- Being athletic makes you special. Sports are everything.
- Having the latest brand name "stuff" is important.

Instead, consider teaching your children these values of the spirit. You will notice how their stress is reduced and their inner strength and resilience is increased:

- Be the best you that you can be.
- You don't have to compete against others. You are cool just being you.
- Be proud of your unique strengths.
- You don't need "stuff" to be special.

Rabbi Menachem Mendel Morgensztern of Kotzk (1987 - 1859) more commonly referred to as the Kotzker Rebbe, was a Hasidic leader, well known for his incisive and down-to-earth philosophies and sharp-witted sayings. My favorite quote from Rabbi Mendel tells us, in a rather unique way, to stay true to the essence and spirit of who we are…

PARENTS, TAKE CHARGE!

If I am I, because I am I

And you are you, because you are you

Then I am, and you are

But if I am I, because you are you

And you are you, because I am I

Then I am not, and you are not

APPENDIX

How To Create Your Personal Dream Board.

Remember that the dream board you are creating is about the future you would love to work towards. It is not about your current reality.

You could speak about your dream and describe it to others. It is very important to do that but it is not enough. It is only half the recipe for making a dream come true. The other half is to 'see it' in your mind's eye. To help you make the dream become a reality, your brain needs to see images/ pictures, as well as hear words.

You are going to create an actual visual representation of your personal dream, using this step-by-step process:

1. You will need a large poster board, paper scissors and paper glue.
2. Collect as many magazines as you can – buy some, get from friends or perhaps you have your own collection. These should be magazines that have many pictures showing all aspects of life. Women's magazines are good for this.
3. Sit somewhere peaceful and private with the poster board, glue, scissors and magazines. Play your favorite music softly in the background. It is preferable to sit on the floor if you are comfortable to do this.
4. Page through the magazines and tear out those pictures that "speak to you" about the kind of future you want to create. Don't question why that picture appeals to you – don't analyze it - just tear out those pages with those pictures. You can choose pages that have words that appeal to you as well - but you want to select mostly pictures.

APPENDIX

5. Keep doing this until you have a pile of pages that you have torn out.
6. Take each page in the pile and cut out the picture or words that appeal to you.
7. Spread these out on the floor or on a table – and look for the story they tell. You will find that a story emerges. This is the story of your dream – the kind of life you want for yourself and the things you want to achieve.
8. Now, glue the pictures on the project board. This is your personal dream board.
9. Show your dream board to at least 3 people you care about and tell them what it means. It is important to hear yourself speak about it to others.
10. Put your personal dream board somewhere safe where you can see it every day. Cherish it and look at it often. This sets your intention for the future and is a powerful tool that can inspire you to achieve the great things you dream about.
11. Every time you feel you need a motivational boost, sit quietly with your dream board and visualize yourself achieving this wonderful dream. If you are not near the dream board, get a picture of it in your mind. This will get your healthy chemicals revving!

I wish you much joy and fulfillment. May you achieve your greatest dreams!

ABOUT THE AUTHOR

Dr. Gluckman holds a degree in Clinical Psychology. Her Ph.D thesis, *The Whole Brain Approach to Education* is based on her research in the effect of using both sides of the brain for teaching and learning. She is the author of, *Who's in the Driver's Seat?* and a chapter in *Mission Possible*. She has published extensively in professional journals. Dr. Gluckman speaks at conferences and presents workshops throughout the world. Her programs, *Parents, Take Charge!* and *Teachers Take Charge!* are being used in the USA, South Africa and soon, Ireland. The programs teach parents and educators how to help children of all ages overcome learning, mood and behavior symptoms without medication.

Her career started as a teacher in high school. During this time she opened a tuition center offering additional assistance to students who had difficulty learning. Then followed over a decade in private practice as a clinical psychologist, during which time she became known for her work with stress-related disorders, as well as her whole brain approach to healing. Sandy developed a Stress Management Program for The Cardiac Prevention and Rehabilitation Center in South

Africa. She also established a Pain Clinic as part of the University of Witwatersrand Dental School.

Dr. Gluckman has also worn a leadership and strategic development hat. She consulted to business leaders around the globe. She taught the Leadership Development program for the Executive MBA Program at Texas Women's University, The University of Dallas Graduate School of Management and the University of Witwatersrand Business School in Johannesburg. Sandy lives in Dallas with her husband. She is now focusing exclusively on her *Parents, Take Charge!* and *Teachers, Take Charge!* programs. She invites readers to email her at **sandy@gluckmangroup.com** and to visit her websites:

www.parentstakecharge.com and www.teacherstakecharge.com

Made in the USA
Las Vegas, NV
19 October 2022